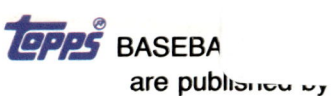 

BASEBALL CARDS

Text by
Bill Shannon

PRICE STERN SLOAN

Los Angeles

Published by Price Stern Sloan, Inc.
360 North La Cienega Boulevard, Los Angeles, California 90048

ISBN 0-8431-2462-8

Officially licensed by Major League Baseball

Official Licensee

© 1988 MLBPA
© MSA

An MBKA Production

Printed and bound in Hong Kong.

TEAM LEADERS

Home Runs

1961 - Harmon Killebrew (46)
1962 - Harmon Killebrew (48)
1963 - Harmon Killebrew (45)
1964 - Harmon Killebrew (49)
1965 - Harmon Killebrew (25)
1966 - Harmon Killebrew (39)
1967 - Harmon Killebrew (44)
1968 - Bob Allison (22)
1969 - Harmon Killebrew (49)
1970 - Harmon Killebrew (41)
1971 - Harmon Killebrew (28)
1972 - Harmon Killebrew (26)
1973 - Bobby Darwin (18)
1974 - Bobby Darwin (25)
1975 - Dan Ford (15)
1976 - Dan Ford (20)
1977 - Larry Hisle (28)
1978 - Roy Smalley (19)
1979 - Roy Smalley (24)
1980 - John Castino (13)
1981 - Roy Smalley (7)
1982 - Gary Ward (28)
1983 - Tom Brunansky (28)
1984 - Tom Brunansky (32)
1985 - Tom Brunansky (27)
1986 - Gary Gaetti (34)
1987 - Kent Hrbek (34)
1988 - Gary Gaetti (28)

Year-by-Year Batting Leaders

Runs Batted In

Harmon Killebrew (122)
Harmon Killebrew (126)
Harmon Killebrew (96)
Harmon Killebrew (111)
Tony Oliva (98)
Harmon Killebrew (110)
Harmon Killebrew (113)
Tony Oliva (68)
Harmon Killebrew (140)
Harmon Killebrew (113)
Harmon Killebrew (119)
Bobby Darwin (80)
Tony Oliva (92)
Bobby Darwin (94)
Rod Carew (80)
Larry Hisle (96)
Larry Hisle (119)
Dan Ford (82)
Roy Smalley (95)
John Castino (64)
Mickey Hatcher (37)
Kent Hrbek (92)
Gary Ward (88)
Kent Hrbek (107)
Kent Hrbek (93)
Gary Gaetti (108)
Gary Gaetti (109)
Kirby Puckett (121)

Batting Average

Earl Battey (.302)
Rich Rollins (.298)
Rich Rollins (.307)
Tony Oliva (.323)
Tony Oliva (.321)
Tony Oliva (.307)
Rod Carew (.292)
Tony Oliva (.289)
Rod Carew (.332)
Tony Oliva (.325)
Tony Oliva (.337)
Rod Carew (.318)
Rod Carew (.350)
Rod Carew (.364)
Rod Carew (.359)
Rod Carew (.331)
Rod Carew (.388)
Rod Carew (.333)
Ken Landreaux (.305)
John Castino (.302)
John Castino (.268)
Kent Hrbek (.301)
Kent Hrbek (.297)
Kent Hrbek (.311)
Kirby Puckett (.288)
Kirby Puckett (.328)
Kirby Puckett (.332)
Kirby Puckett (.356)

Compiled by Bill Haber.

Year-by-Year Pitching Leaders

Year	Wins	Strikeouts	Earned Run Average
1961	Camilo Pascual (15)	Camilo Pascual (221)	Camilo Pascual (3.46)
1962	Camilo Pascual (20)	Camilo Pascual (206)	Jim Kaat (3.14)
1963	Camilo Pascual (21)	Camilo Pascual (202)	Camilo Pascual (2.47)
1964	Jim Kaat (17)	Camilo Pascual (213)	Jim Kaat (3.22)
1965	Jim "Mudcat" Grant (21)	Jim Kaat (154)	Jim Perry (2.63)
1966	Jim Kaat (25)	Jim Kaat (205)	Jim Perry (2.54)
1967	Dean Chance (20)	Dean Chance (220)	Jim Merritt (2.53)
1968	Dean Chance (16)	Dean Chance (234)	Dean Chance (2.53)
1969	Dave Boswell, Jim Perry (20)	Dave Boswell (190)	Jim Perry (2.82)
1970	Jim Perry (24)	Tom Hall (184)	Jim Perry (3.03)
1971	Jim Perry (17)	Bert Blyleven (224)	Bert Blyleven (2.82)
1972	Bert Blyleven (17)	Bert Blyleven (228)	Ray Corbin (2.61)
1973	Bert Blyleven (20)	Bert Blyleven (258)	Bert Blyleven (2.52)
1974	Bert Blyleven (17)	Bert Blyleven (249)	Bert Blyleven (2.66)
1975	Jim Hughes (16)	Bert Blyleven (233)	Bert Blyleven (3.00)
1976	Bill Campbell (17)	Dave Goltz (133)	Bill Campbell (3.00)
1977	Dave Goltz (20)	Dave Goltz (186)	Dave Goltz (3.36)
1978	Dave Goltz (15)	Roger Erickson (121)	Dave Goltz (2.50)
1979	Jerry Koosman (20)	Jerry Koosman (157)	Jerry Koosman (3.38)
1980	Jerry Koosman (16)	Jerry Koosman (149)	Roger Erickson (3.25)
1981	Pete Redfern (9)	Pete Redfern (77)	Fernando Arroyo (3.94)
1982	Bobby Castillo (13)	Brad Havens (129)	Bobby Castillo (3.66)
1983	Ken Schrom (15)	Frank Viola (127)	Ken Schrom (3.71)
1984	Frank Viola (18)	Frank Viola (149)	Frank Viola (3.21)
1985	Frank Viola (18)	Frank Viola (135)	Frank Viola (4.09)
1986	Bert Blyleven (17)	Bert Blyleven (215)	Bert Blyleven (4.01)
1987	Frank Viola (17)	Frank Viola (197)	Frank Viola (2.90)
1988	Frank Viola (24)	Frank Viola (193)	Allan Anderson (2.45)

Most Valuable Twin

1961 - Harmon Killebrew
1962 - Vic Power
1963 - Earl Battey
1964 - Tony Oliva
1965 - Zoilo Versalles
1966 - Harmon Killebrew
1967 - Harmon Killebrew
1968 - Cesar Tovar
1969 - Harmon Killebrew
1970 - Harmon Killebrew
1971 - Leo Cardenas
1972 - Rod Carew
1973 - Rod Carew
1974 - Rod Carew
1975 - Rod Carew
1976 - Rod Carew
1977 - Rod Carew
1978 - Roy Smalley
1979 - Roy Smalley
1980 - John Castino
1981 - Doug Corbett
1982 - Gary Ward
1983 - John Castino
1984 - Kent Hrbek
1985 - Kirby Puckett
1986 - Kirby Puckett
1987 - Jeff Reardon

1952

During the period when the team was known as the Washington Nationals, it didn't perform much better than when it was known as the Senators. A fifth-place (78-76) finish only 17 games out was considered a major success this season. Spending almost two-thirds of the season in the first division, the Nats reached third in early September but then struggled through a 12-13 final month to finish fifth.

The generally upbeat season for manager Bucky Harris' team resulted partly from a May 3 trade with the Yankees that sent outfielder Irv Noren to New York for outfielder Jackie Jensen and pitcher Frank (Specs) Shea. Jensen hit .286 with 10 homers and 80 RBIs for 144 games in Washington (.280 overall including 7 games with the Yankees) and Pete Runnels hit .285 with 64 RBIs. Shea was 11-7 while Bob Porterfield led the staff with 13-14 and a 2.73 ERA (seventh best in the league) and Connie Marrero was 11-8.

FLOYD BAKER

JIM BUSBY

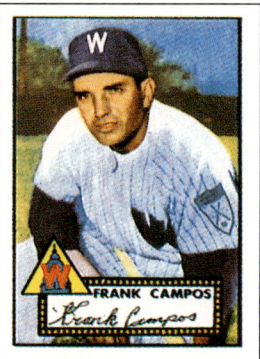
FRANK CAMPOS

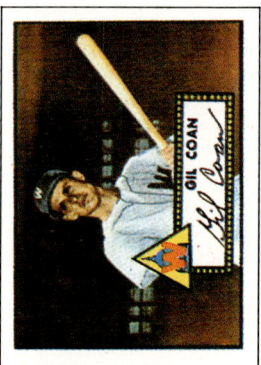
GIL COAN

MICKEY GRASSO

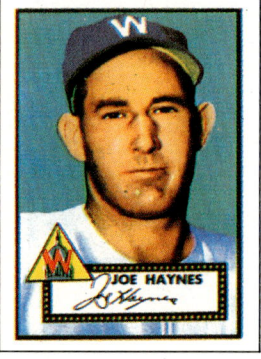
JOE HAYNES

SID HUDSON

DON JOHNSON

CLYDE KLUTTZ

CONNIE MARRERO

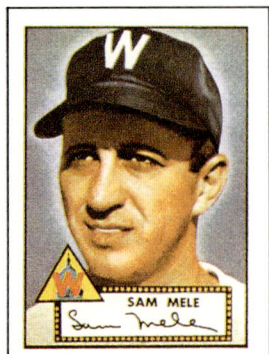

SAM MELE

CASS MICHAELS

IRV NOREN

BOB PORTERFIELD

SHERRY ROBERTSON

BOB ROSS

Floyd Robert Ross

JAMES E. RUNNELS

AL SIMA

LOU SLEATER

TOM UPTON

MICKEY VERNON

EDDIE YOST

1953

Another fifth-place finish (76-76), 23 ½ games behind the pennant-winning Yankees, produced a couple of outstanding individual highlights. First baseman Mickey Vernon became the first (and only) Senator ever to lead the league in batting more than once when he hit .337 to win his second batting title (he had won it in 1946); he also finished second in the league with 115 RBIs, leading the team with 15 home runs. Outfielder Jim Busby hit .312 with 82 RBIs while third baseman Eddie Yost (.272) led the league with 123 walks. But the season was damaged early when Gil Coan fractured his leg in spring training and hit only .196 in 68 games.

Bob Porterfield had another outstanding season with a 22-10 record (tops in wins in the league), 24 complete games (also first) and 9 shutouts. Frank Shea was 12-7, Chuck Stobbs 11-8 and Walt Masterson 10-12. Attendance at Griffith Stadium was 595,594, a drop of almost 104,000 from 1952.

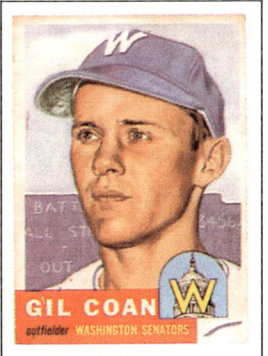

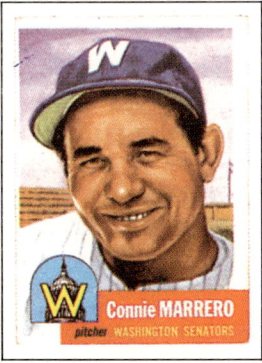

PETE RUNNELS
shortstop WASHINGTON SENATORS

FRANK SHEA
pitcher WASHINGTON SENATORS

AL SIMA
pitcher WASHINGTON SENATORS

LOU SLEATER
pitcher WASHINGTON SENATORS

CHUCK STOBBS
pitcher WASHINGTON SENATORS

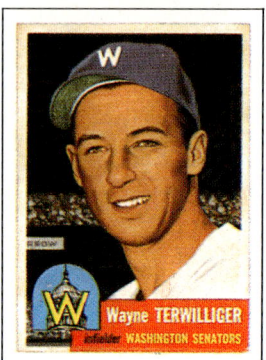
Wayne TERWILLIGER
infielder WASHINGTON SENATORS

1954

A season that began with a 6-6 April ended with a soggy sixth-place standing and a 66-88 record, 45 games out. Two days before the season ended, Bucky Harris was told he would not be back as manager, ending his third and final tour as Washington pilot. His third tenure, beginning in 1950, produced a 349-419 record; overall Harris was 1,336-1,416, having managed the Senators to pennants in 1924 and 1925.

Bob Porterfield, despite tying for the league lead with 21 complete games, was 13-15, Johnny Schmitz was 11-8 and Dean Stone 12-10. But the big disappointment was Frank (Specs) Shea who lost 20 pounds over the winter and then lost his first 8 decisions during the season, finishing at 2-9 with a 6.21 ERA.

With the leftfield wall at Griffith Stadium shortened from 405 feet to 386, Roy Sievers enjoyed a fine power year with 24 homers and 102 RBIs although he hit just .232. Mickey Vernon (.290) set a Washington record for lefthand hitters, slugging 20 homers. He had 97 RBIs. Jim Busby hit .298 to lead the team.

JOE HAYNES
coach WASHINGTON SENATORS

JERRY LANE
pitcher WASHINGTON SENATORS

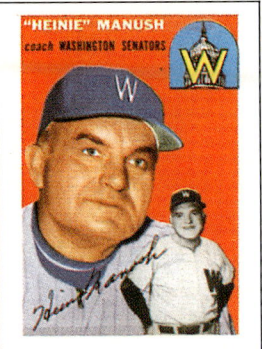

"HEINIE" MANUSH
coach WASHINGTON SENATORS

BOB OLDIS
catcher WASHINGTON SENATORS

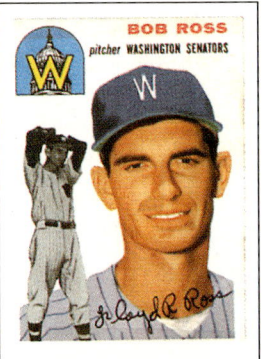

BOB ROSS
pitcher WASHINGTON SENATORS

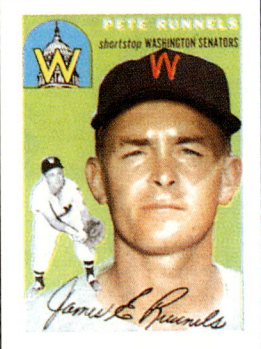

PETE RUNNELS
shortstop WASHINGTON SENATORS

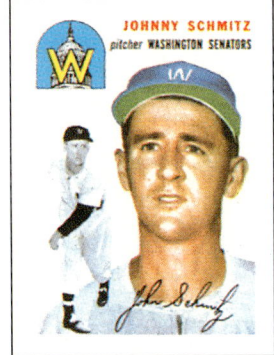

JOHNNY SCHMITZ
pitcher WASHINGTON SENATORS

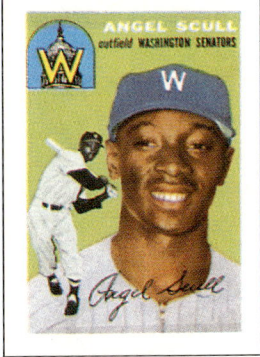

ANGEL SCULL
outfield WASHINGTON SENATORS

ROY SIEVERS
outfield WASHINGTON SENATORS

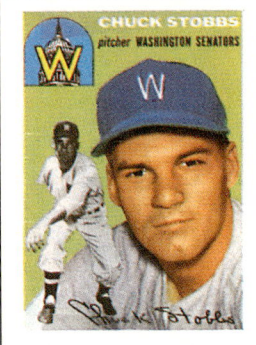

CHUCK STOBBS
pitcher WASHINGTON SENATORS

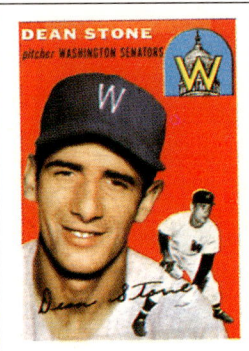

DEAN STONE
pitcher WASHINGTON SENATORS

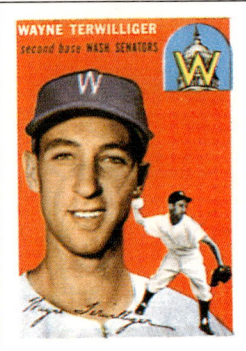

WAYNE TERWILLIGER
second base WASH SENATORS

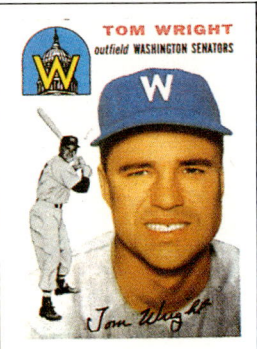

TOM WRIGHT
outfield WASHINGTON SENATORS

1955

Under new manager Chuck Dressen the Senators (as they once again were officially known) plunged into the cellar, finishing eighth with a 53-101 record, 43 games behind, and drew a meager 425,238 to Griffith Stadium.

While the team had no winning months, Mickey Vernon continued his fine hitting, batting .301 with 14 homers and 85 RBIs. Roy Sievers (.271) hit 25 homers and had 106 RBIs and Pete Runnels batted .284. In June, Jim Busby was traded to Chicago for three players. Mickey McDermott (10-10) had the best record among the pitchers as Bob Porterfield slumped to 10-17 with a 4.45 ERA.

On Oct. 27 Clark Griffith died. Griffith had been with the Senators since 1912 and the major owner since 1920. His adopted son, Calvin Griffith, took over and, on Nov. 8, traded Vernon to Boston for five players including Tex Clevenger.

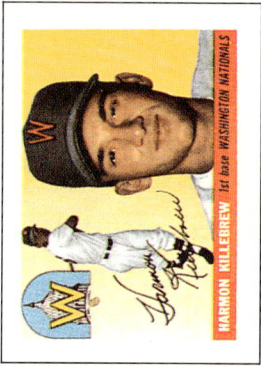

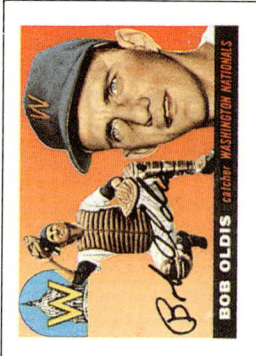
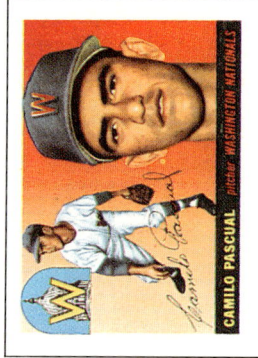

 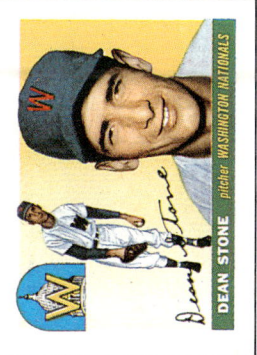  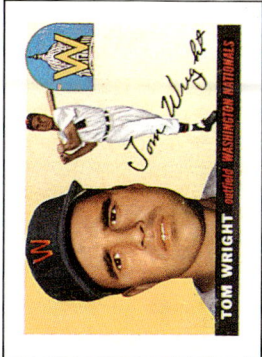

1956

With leftfield shortened once again by new club president Calvin Griffith from 386 feet to 350 down the line, the Senators put on a power display that easily broke team records. With Roy Sievers belting 29 and new slugger Jim Lemon 27, Washington collected 112 homers, surpassing the former club mark of 85 set in 1938. Sievers (.253) had 95 RBIs and Lemon (.271) led the club with 96 while Pete Runnels (.310) added 76. Lemon hit 21 homers at Griffith Stadium, most ever there by one hitter up to that time. He also set a major league record with 138 strikeouts.

Despite the excitement of the home runs, the season had a very familiar look. After a 7-6 April the Senators fell out of the race with 9-19 May. The team finished by losing 21 of its last 26 and 13 of the last 14, escaping the cellar only because Kansas City was 45 games out. Washington (59-95) was 38. Chuck Stobbs (15-15) led the pitchers while Pete Ramos was 12-10.

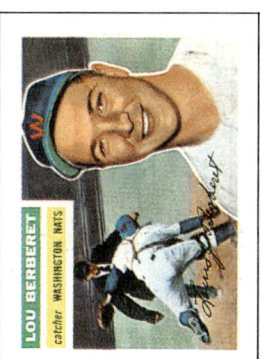 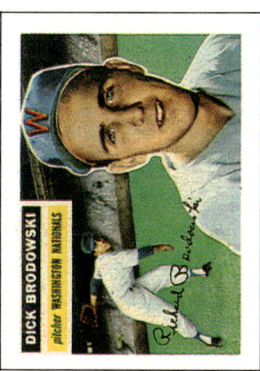 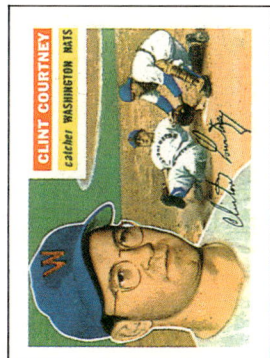 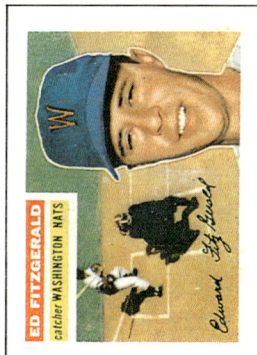

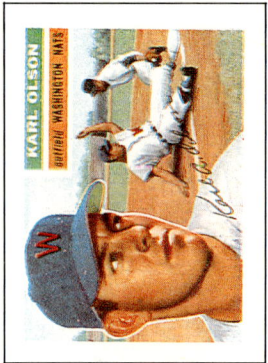

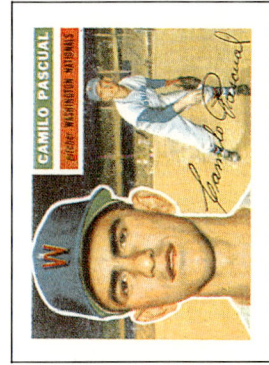

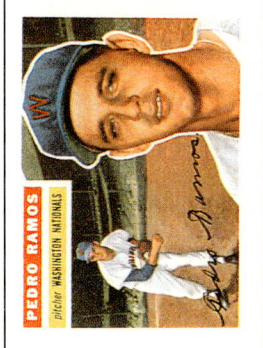

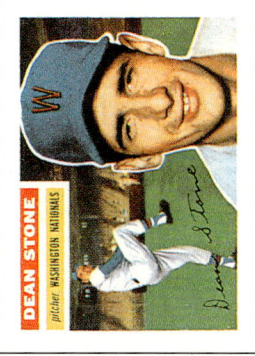
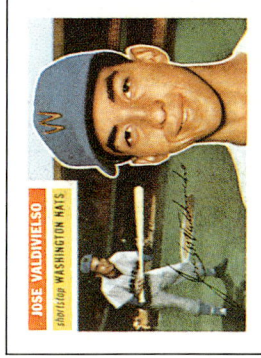

1957

Chuck Dressen began his third season as manager but after the team lost 16 of its first 20 he was fired on May 7. New manager Cookie Lavagetto was unable to effect any miracle cures, however, and the Senators finished last with a 55-99 record, 43 games out. Roy Sievers had perhaps his best all-around season, hitting .301 with league-leading home run (42) and RBI (114) totals. He was the first Senators player ever to lead the league in home runs.

One of the highlights of the season came on June 27 when a "lucky charm night" was held to help Chuck Stobbs stop a 16-game personal losing streak. Stobbs (then 0-11) won, 6-3, over Cleveland as 9,462 fans cheered him on aided by 3,200 charms including rabbit's feet and horseshoes. Pedro Ramos was the winningest pitcher with a 12-16 record, Camilio Pascual was 8-17. Stobbs won 8 of his last 17 decisions to end at 8-20 and Russ Kemmerer was 7-11 after being acquired from Boston.

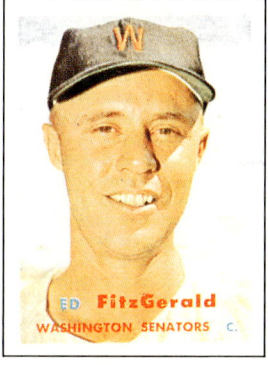

JIM Lemon
WASHINGTON SENATORS O.F.

LYLE Luttrell
WASHINGTON SENATORS S.S.

KARL Olson
WASHINGTON SENATORS O.F.

ERNIE Oravetz
WASHINGTON SENATORS O.F.

CAMILO Pascual
WASHINGTON SENATORS P.

HERB Plews
WASHINGTON SENATORS 2nd B.

PEDRO Ramos
WASHINGTON SENATORS P.

PETE Runnels
WASHINGTON SENATORS 1st B.

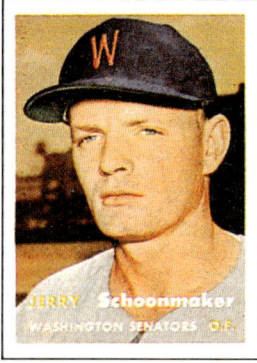

JERRY Schoonmaker
WASHINGTON SENATORS O.F.

ROY Sievers
WASHINGTON SENATORS O.F.

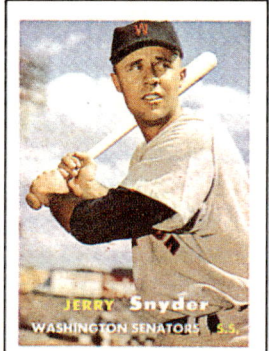

JERRY Snyder
WASHINGTON SENATORS S.S.

CHUCK Stobbs
WASHINGTON SENATORS P.

FAYE Throneberry
WASHINGTON SENATORS O.F.

JOSE Valdivielso
WASHINGTON SENATORS S.S.

BOB Wiesler
WASHINGTON SENATORS P.

EDDIE Yost
WASHINGTON SENATORS 3rd B.

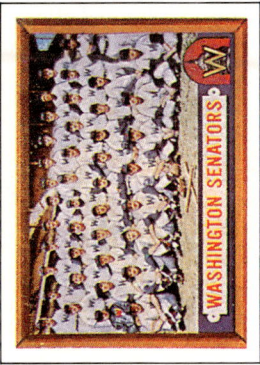

1958

With Cookie Lavagetto beginning his first full season as manager, the Senators got off to a strong early start, standing second until mid-May when Roy Sievers injured his leg. By mid-June the team was eight and finished there with a 61-93 record, 31 games behind. Sievers came back from the injury to hit .295 with 39 homers (second in the league) and 108 RBIs. Little Albie Pearson hit .275 and two youngsters made their appearances. Bob Allison hit .200 in 11 games and Harmon Killebrew .194 in 13.

Club president Calvin Griffith, later called to testify before Congress about the matter, discussed moving the team to Minneapolis but was rebuffed by his fellow owners at the All-Star Game meeting. After the league meeting July 6, an offer from Minneapolis was withdrawn.

Pedro Ramos again led the pitchers with a 14-14 record, Tex Clevenger was 9-9 and Camilio Pascual 8-12. Coming out of the bullpen, Dick Hyde emerged as a new star with a 10-3 record in 53 appearances.

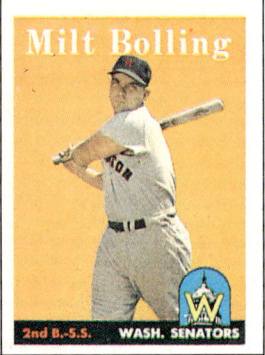

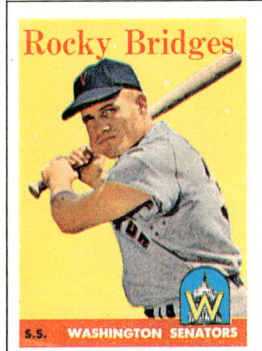

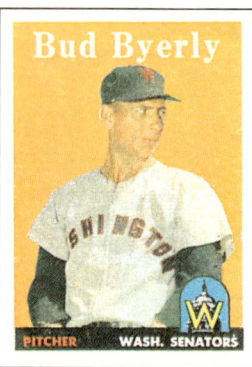
Bud Byerly — PITCHER — WASH. SENATORS

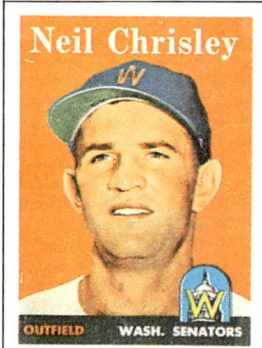
Neil Chrisley — OUTFIELD — WASH. SENATORS

Tex Clevenger — PITCHER — WASH. SENATORS

Clint Courtney — CATCHER — WASH. SENATORS

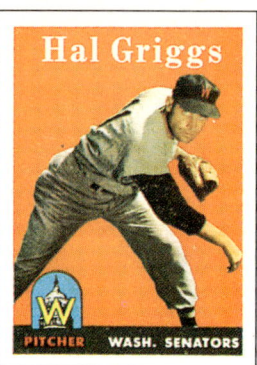
Hal Griggs — PITCHER — WASH. SENATORS

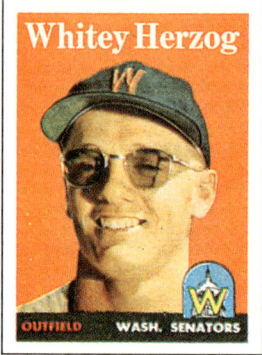
Whitey Herzog — OUTFIELD — WASH. SENATORS

Dick Hyde — PITCHER — WASH. SENATORS

Russ Kemmerer — PITCHER — WASH. SENATORS

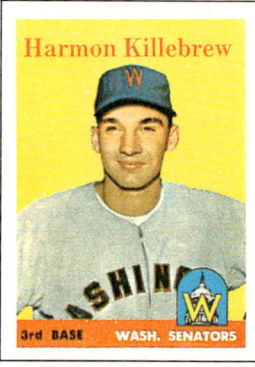
Harmon Killebrew — 3rd BASE — WASH. SENATORS

Steve Korcheck — CATCHER — WASH. SENATORS

Jim Lemon — OUTFIELD — WASH. SENATORS

Ralph Lumenti — PITCHER — WASH. SENATORS

Bob Malkmus — 2nd BASE — WASH. SENATORS

Camilo Pascual — PITCHER — WASH. SENATORS

Albie Pearson — OUTFIELD — WASH. SENATORS

Herb Plews — 2nd B. — WASH. SENATORS

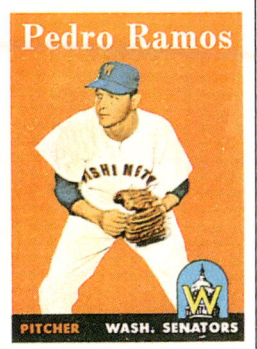
Pedro Ramos — PITCHER — WASH. SENATORS

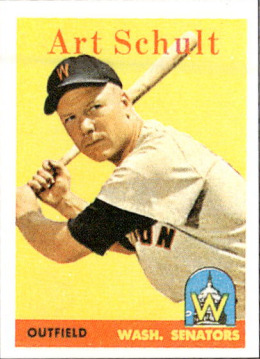
Art Schult — OUTFIELD — WASH. SENATORS

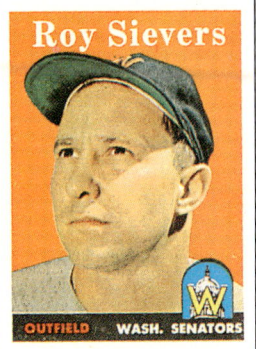
Roy Sievers — OUTFIELD — WASH. SENATORS

Chuck Stobbs — PITCHER — WASH. SENATORS

Bobby Usher — OUTFIELD — WASH. SENATORS

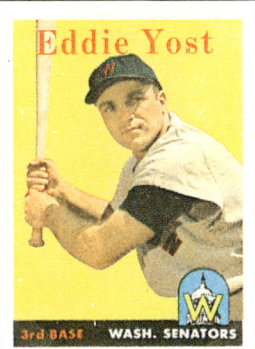
Eddie Yost — 3rd BASE — WASH. SENATORS

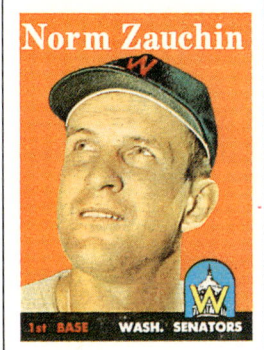
Norm Zauchin — 1st BASE — WASH. SENATORS

1959

Although the Senators were once again eighth (63-91), the fans had more fun than usual at Griffith Stadium and there were more fans than usual. After four seasons of attendance under 500,000, the total jumped to 615,372 as the Senators slammed a record 163 home runs, eclipsing a three-year-old record, with Harmon Killebrew leading the way. Killebrew had 31 homers by July 15 and Senators fans were wondering if he could challenge Babe Ruth's record. But he finished with 42, good enough for a tie for first in the league though far from the record. Killebrew (.242) drove in 105 runs. Jim Lemon (.279) hit 33 homers with 100 RBIs, Bob Allison (.261) had 30 with 85 RBIs and Roy Sievers (.242) hit 21 with 49 RBIs despite injuries.

Camilio Pascual added to the excitement with a 17-10 record including 6 shutouts and a 2.64 ERA. Pedro Ramos was 13-19 and Jack Fischer 9-11. An 18-game losing streak that ended on Aug. 5 killed the chances of rising above last place.

ted abernathy

WASHINGTON SENATORS
PITCHER

The Sporting News
ROOKIE STARS OF 1959

BOB ALLISON
SENATORS   OUTFIELD

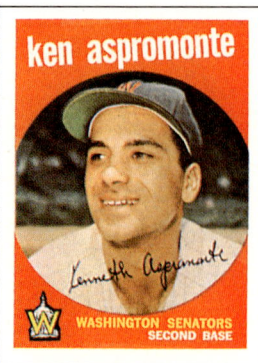

ken aspromonte

WASHINGTON SENATORS
SECOND BASE

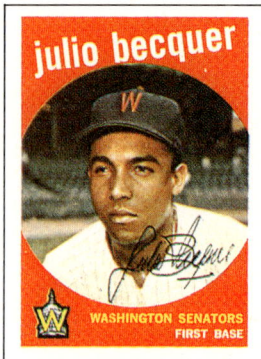

julio becquer

WASHINGTON SENATORS
FIRST BASE

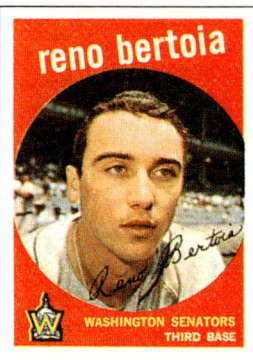

reno bertoia

WASHINGTON SENATORS
THIRD BASE

tex clevenger

WASHINGTON SENATORS
PITCHER

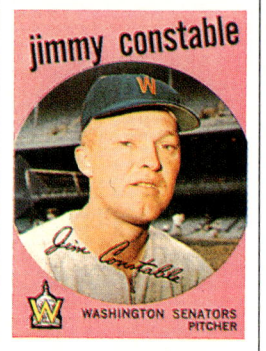

jimmy constable

WASHINGTON SENATORS
PITCHER

clint courtney

WASHINGTON SENATORS
CATCHER

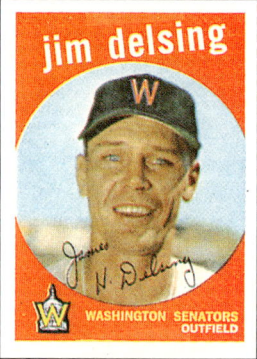

jim delsing

WASHINGTON SENATORS
OUTFIELD

The Sporting News
ROOKIE STARS OF 1959

DAN DOBBEK
SENATORS   OUTFIELD

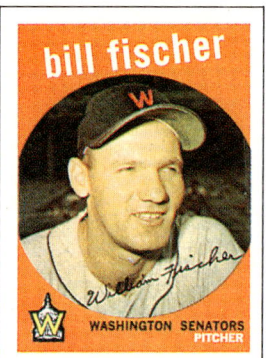

bill fischer

WASHINGTON SENATORS
PITCHER

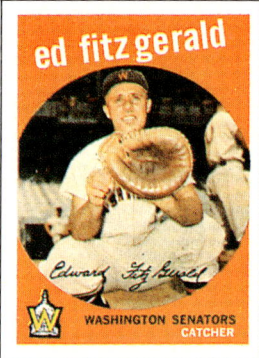

ed fitzgerald

WASHINGTON SENATORS
CATCHER

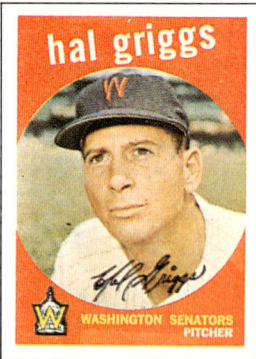

hal griggs

WASHINGTON SENATORS
PITCHER

dick hyde

WASHINGTON SENATORS
PITCHER

russ kemmerer

WASHINGTON SENATORS
PITCHER

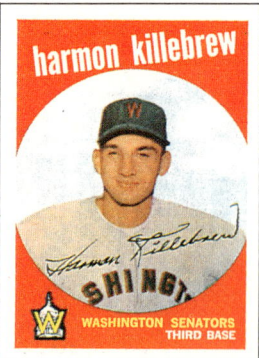

harmon killebrew

WASHINGTON SENATORS
THIRD BASE

steve korcheck

WASHINGTON SENATORS
CATCHER

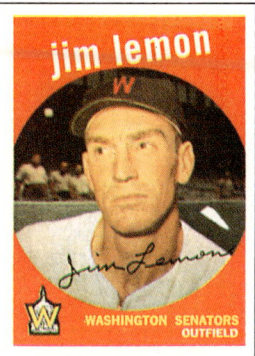

jim lemon

WASHINGTON SENATORS
OUTFIELD

ralph lumenti

WASHINGTON SENATORS
PITCHER

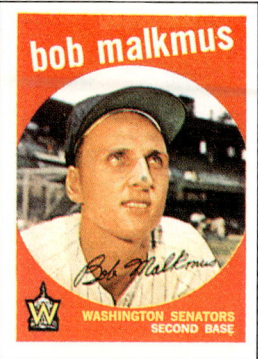

bob malkmus

WASHINGTON SENATORS
SECOND BASE

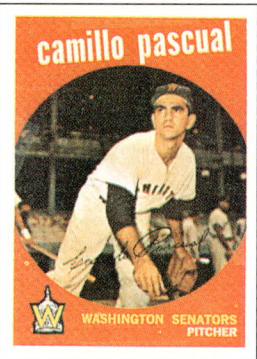

camillo pascual

WASHINGTON SENATORS
PITCHER

albie pearson

WASHINGTON SENATORS
OUTFIELD

herb plews

WASHINGTON SENATORS
SECOND BASE—THIRD BASE

j. w. porter

WASHINGTON SENATORS
CATCHER—OUTFIELD

pedro ramos

WASHINGTON SENATORS
PITCHER

john romonosky

WASHINGTON SENATORS
PITCHER

ron samford

WASHINGTON SENATORS
SHORTSTOP

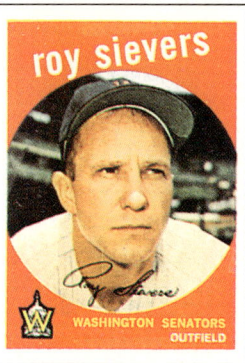

roy sievers

WASHINGTON SENATORS
OUTFIELD

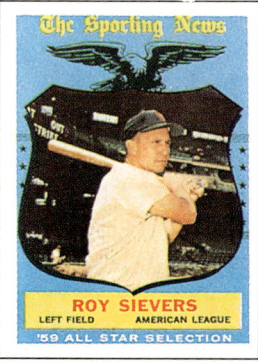

The Sporting News

ROY SIEVERS

LEFT FIELD   AMERICAN LEAGUE
'59 ALL STAR SELECTION

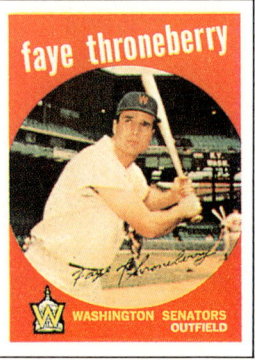

faye throneberry

WASHINGTON SENATORS
OUTFIELD

vito valentinetti

WASHINGTON SENATORS
PITCHER

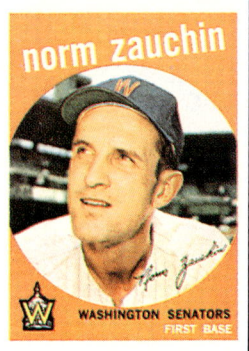

norm zauchin

WASHINGTON SENATORS
FIRST BASE

1960

Finally things began to improve for the Senators as they rose to fifth (73-81), 24 games back, and missed fourth by losing 15 of their last 18 games. Before the late collapse the team was over .500 on Sept. 18 (70-66).

Jim Lemon batted .269 with a career-high 38 homers and 100 RBIs. Harmon Killebrew had only 3 homers through July 17 but then caught fire to finish with 31 and 80 RBIs. Camilio Pascual missed a month with a sore arm but was still 12-8 with a 3.02 ERA. Chuck Stobbs was 12-7, Pedro Ramos 11-18 and Don Lee 8-7.

But the big news came on Oct. 26 in New York when Calvin Griffith received permission to transfer the team to Minnesota and a new expansion franchise was granted for Washington. Economics motivated the move as Griffith pointed out that he was guaranteed $500,000 for his television rights in Minnesota and that he had earned only $180,000 in 1960 in Washington.

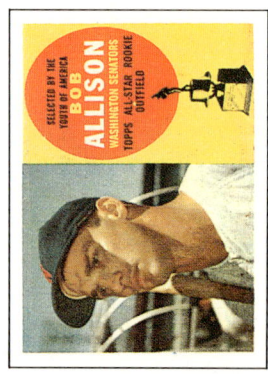
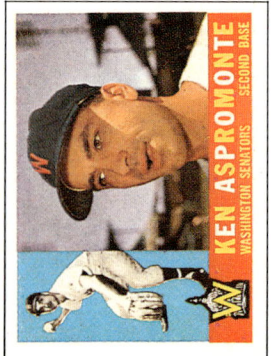
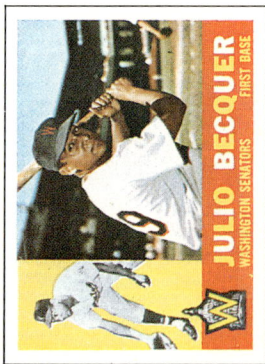

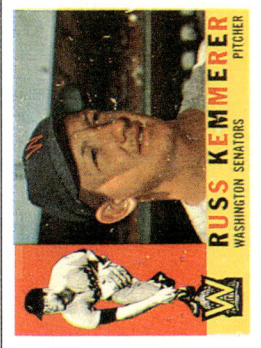
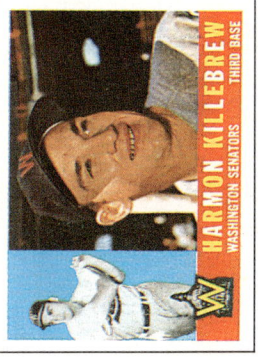

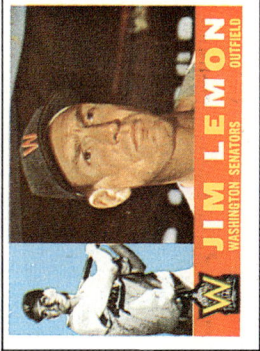

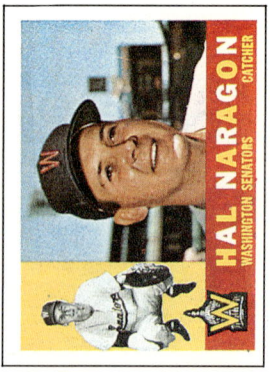

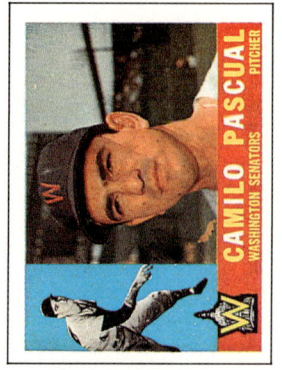

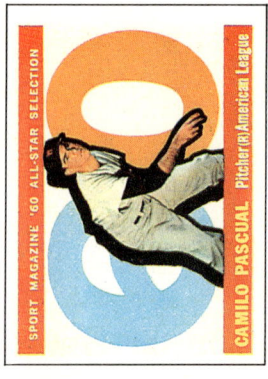

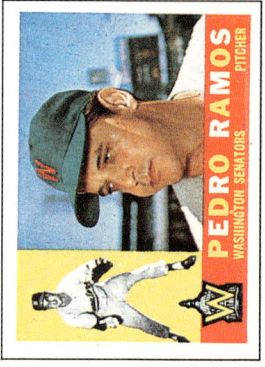

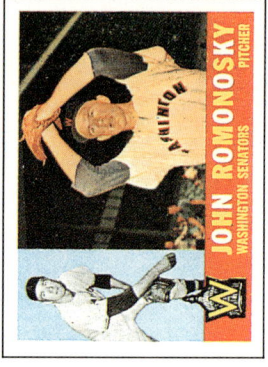

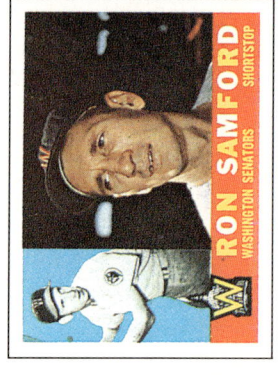

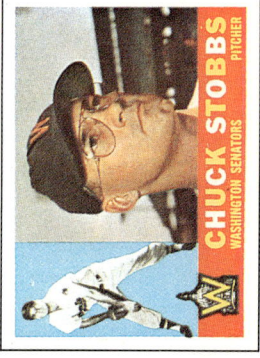

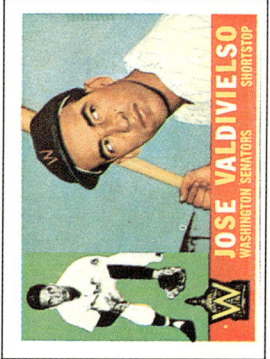

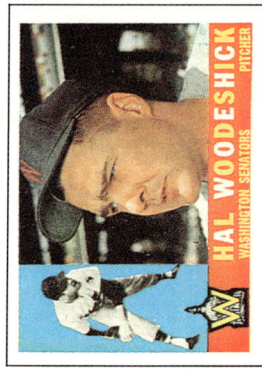

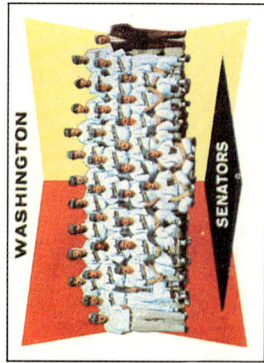

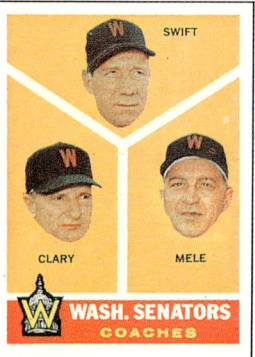

1961

A new location and a new stadium gave the team a temporary lift as the new Minnesota Twins started life by winning 9 of their first 12 games and moving into first place. However, the burst soon faded and on June 13 Cookie Lavagetto was fired as manager and replaced by Sam Mele. On June 6 Lavagetto was given a week off with the team during a slide that included 13 straight losses and 18 in 19 games. After he returned on June 13 things didn't improve and he was dismissed. The team (70-90) finished seventh.

Young catcher Earl Battey hit .302 with 17 homers and 55 RBIs while Harmon Killebrew (.288) hit 46 homers with 122 RBIs. Bob Allison (.245) had 29 homers and 105 RBIs.

Minnesota fans, who turned out 1,256,723 strong for their first taste of major league baseball at Metropolitan Stadium, also saw Camilio Pascual lead the league with 221 strikeouts en route to a 15-16 season with 8 shutouts and a 3.46 ERA. Jack Kralick was 13-11, Jim Kaat 9-17 and Pedro Ramos 11-20.

LENNY GREEN
Outfield — Minnesota Twins

JIM KAAT
Pitcher — Minnesota Twins

HARMON KILLEBREW
First Base-Third Base — Minnesota Twins

JACK KRALICK
Pitcher — Minnesota Twins

HARRY LAVAGETTO
Mgr. — Minnesota Twins

DON LEE
Pitcher — Minnesota Twins

JIM LEMON
Outfield — Minnesota Twins

RALPH LUMENTI
Pitcher — Minnesota Twins

DON MINCHER
First Base — Minnesota Twins

RAY MOORE
Pitcher — Minnesota Twins

HAL NARAGON
Catcher — Minnesota Twins

PEDRO RAMOS
Pitcher — Minnesota Twins

1961 ROOKIE

TED SADOWSKI
Pitcher — Minnesota Twins

CHUCK STOBBS
Pitcher — Minnesota Twins

JOSE VALDIVIELSO
Shortstop — Minnesota Twins

ELMER VALO
Outfield — Minnesota Twins

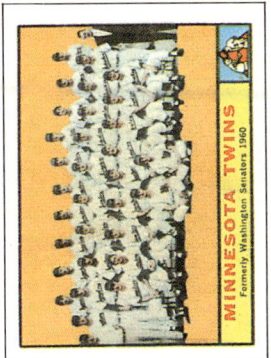

1962

A week before the season, the Twins traded veteran pitcher Pedro Ramos to Cleveland for first baseman Vic Power and pitcher Dick Stigman. The deal turned out to have a very positive impact as the team leaped up to second (91-71) only 5 games behind the champion Yankees.

Power hit .290 with 16 homers and 63 RBIs while playing a skillful first base. Other new infielders — second baseman Bernie Allen (.269 with 12 homers) and third baseman Rich Rollins (.298 with 16 homers and 96 RBIs)—also helped the resurgence. Harmon Killebrew had another powerhouse season, batting only .243 but leading the league in homers (48) and RBIs (126) and Bob Allison hit .266 with 29 homers and 102 RBIs.

Minnesota fans got their first no-hitter as Jack Kralick defeated Kansas City 1-0, on Aug. 26. Kralick was 12-11, Stigman 12-5, Jim Kaat 18-14 and Camilio Pascual 20-11 with a 3.31 ERA. Ray Moore was 8-3 in 49 relief appearances.

JIM
KAAT
MINN. TWINS P

HARMON
KILLEBREW
MINN. TWINS 1B-OF

KILLEBREW SENDS ONE INTO ORBIT

JACK
KRALICK
MIN. TWINS PITCHER

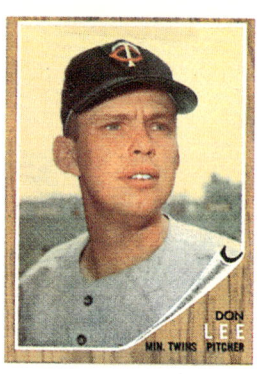

DON
LEE
MIN. TWINS PITCHER

JIM
LEMON
MIN. TWINS OF

BILLY
MARTIN
MINN. TWINS 2B

SAM
MELE
MIN. TWINS MGR.

DON
MINCHER
MINN. TWINS 1B

RAY
MOORE
MINN. TWINS P

HAL
NARAGON
MIN. TWINS CATCHER

CAMILO
PASCUAL
MINN. TWINS P

BILL
PLEIS
MIN. TWINS PITCHER

VIC
POWER
MIN. TWINS 1B

AL
SCHROLL
MINN. TWINS P

LEE
STANGE
MIN. TWINS PITCHER

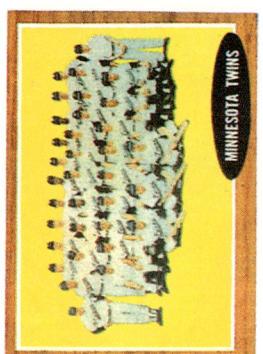

1963

Ringing up the second highest home run total of any team in major league history (225), the Twins once again stayed in the pennant race most of the season but finally finished third (91-70), 13 games out.

Harmon Killebrew led the league with 45 homers, hitting .258 with 96 RBIs. Bob Allison hit 35, batting .271 with 91 RBIs. Rookie Jimmy Hall (.260) hit 33 homers with 80 RBIs and Earl Battey (.285) had 26 homers and 84 RBIs. On May 16 the club was 10th (11-20) but then won 21 of 27 to pull within 2 games of first place. Then Camilio Pascual pulled a muscle in his shoulder and made only one start in 35 days. Pascual still finished with a 21-9 record but his absence slowed the drive and perhaps cost the Twins a chance to win the title. Minnesota dropped 9 of 10 in early July. Dick Stigman was 15-15, Lee Stange 12-5 and Jim Kaat 10-10. Jim Perry, acquired from Cleveland in early May, was 9-9.

BERNIE
ALLEN
MINNESOTA TWINS 2B

BOB
ALLISON
MINN. TWINS OF

GEORGE
BANKS
MINNESOTA TWINS 3B-OF

EARL
BATTEY
MINNESOTA TWINS C

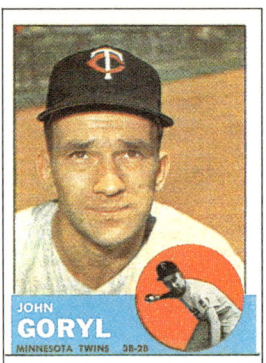
JOHN
GORYL
MINNESOTA TWINS 3B-2B

LENNY
GREEN
MINNESOTA TWINS OF

JIM
KAAT
MINN. TWINS PITCHER

HARMON
KILLEBREW
MINNESOTA TWINS OF

JACK
KRALICK
MINNESOTA TWINS P

JIM
LEMON
MINNESOTA TWINS OF

SAM
MELE
MINNESOTA TWINS MGR.

DON
MINCHER
MINN. TWINS 1B

RAY
MOORE
MINN. TWINS PITCHER

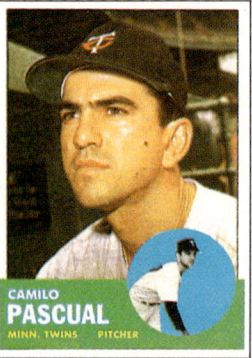
CAMILO
PASCUAL
MINN. TWINS PITCHER

JIM
PERRY
MINNESOTA TWINS P

BILL
PLEIS
MINNESOTA TWINS P

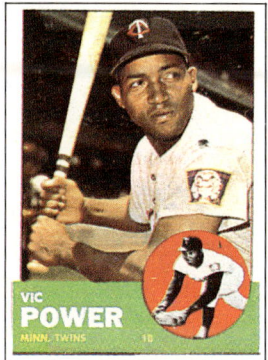

VIC
POWER
MINN. TWINS   1B

RICH
ROLLINS
MINNESOTA TWINS   3b.

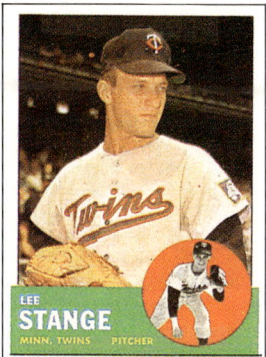

LEE
STANGE
MINN. TWINS   PITCHER

DICK
STIGMAN
MINN. TWINS   PITCHER

FRANK
SULLIVAN
MINN. TWINS   PITCHER

BILL
TUTTLE
MINNESOTA TWINS   OF

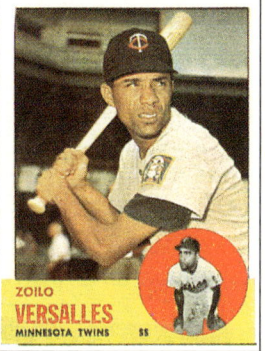

ZOILO
VERSALLES
MINNESOTA TWINS   SS

JERRY
ZIMMERMAN
MINNESOTA TWINS   C

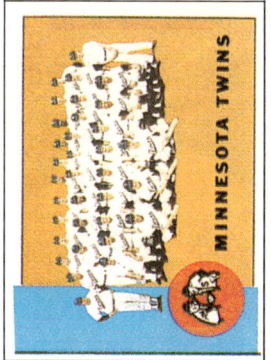

MINNESOTA TWINS

1964

Despite matching the third-best team homer total ever (221) and leading the league in runs scored, Twins had a surprisingly poor season, dropping into a sixth-place tie with a 79-83 record, 20 games out of first. After reaching fourth on June 12, the team lost 14 of 22 and was never again a factor in the race.

Six men on the Twins hit 20 or more home runs with Harmon Killebrew (.270) leading the league for the third straight season with 49 and also driving in 111 runs. Other sluggers were Bob Allison (.287) and rookie Tony Oliva (.323) with 32 each, Jimmy Hall (.282) with 25, Don Mincher (.237) with 23 and shortstop Zoilo Versalles (.259) with 20. Oliva also had 94 RBIs as he became the first rookie ever to win the league batting title, setting records for hits (217) and total bases (374) by a rookie in the process. Jim Kaat, 17-11, was the top pitcher and Camilio Pascual was 15-12 and Jim (Mudcat) Grant 11-9.

TWINS

BERNIE ALLEN 2nd base

TWINS

BOB ALLISON of-1b

TWINS

GEORGE BANKS 3b-of

TWINS

EARL BATTEY catcher

TWINS

BILL DAILEY pitcher

TWINS

BILL FISCHER pitcher

TWINS

JOHN GORYL 3b-2b

TWINS

LENNY GREEN outfield

TWINS

JIMMIE HALL outfield

TWINS

JIM KAAT pitcher

TWINS

HARMON KILLEBREW of

TWINS

SAM MELE manager

TWINS

DON MINCHER 1st base

TWINS

CAMILO PASCUAL pitcher

TWINS

JIM PERRY pitcher

TWINS

BILL PLEIS pitcher

TWINS

VIC POWER 1st base

TWINS

GARRY ROGGENBURK p

TWINS

JIM ROLAND pitcher

TWINS

RICH ROLLINS 3rd base

TWINS

LEE STANGE pitcher

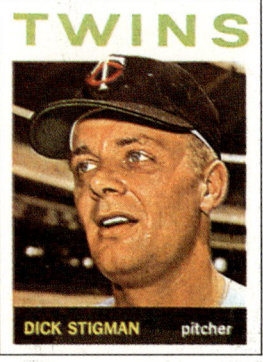

TWINS

DICK STIGMAN pitcher

TWINS

ZOILO VERSALLES ss

TWINS

JERRY ZIMMERMAN c

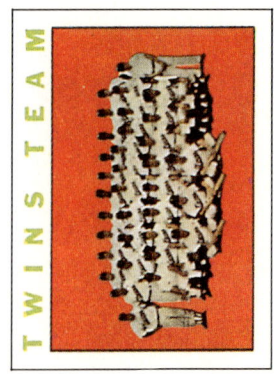

1965

Withstanding a rash of injuries to such key men as Camilio Pascual, Harmon Killebrew, Tony Oliva and Earl Battey, the Twins still won the pennant with a 102-60 record, finishing 7 games in front. Minnesota thus became only the third team since 1946 to win an American League pennant besides the Yankees. Chicago won in 1959 and Cleveland twice (1948 and 1954).

Shortstop Zoilo Versalles won the Most Valuable Player award for his season of superb fielding plus a .273 batting average, 19 homers and 77 RBIs. Oliva hit .321 with 16 homers and 98 RBIs, Killebrew hit .269 with 25 homers and 75 RBIs, Jim Hall hit .285 with 20 homers and 86 RBIs while Bob Allison (23) and Don Mincher (22) combined for 45 more homers.

Jim (Mudcat) Grant was 21-7 and won Games 1 and 6 in the World Series but the Twins were beaten by the Los Angeles Dodgers in 7 games as Jim Kaat (18-11 during the season) was bested by Sandy Koufax, 2-0, in the deciding seventh game.

PITCHER
JERRY FOSNOW

PITCHER
JIM GRANT

OUTFIELD
JIMMIE HALL

PITCHER
JIM KATT

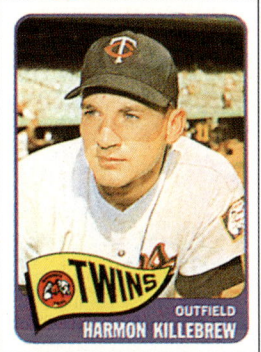

OUTFIELD
HARMON KILLEBREW

PITCHER
JOHNNY KLIPPSTEIN

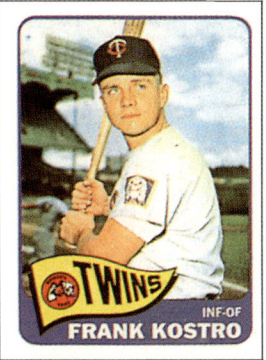

INF-OF
FRANK KOSTRO

MANAGER
SAM MELE

1st BASE
DON MINCHER

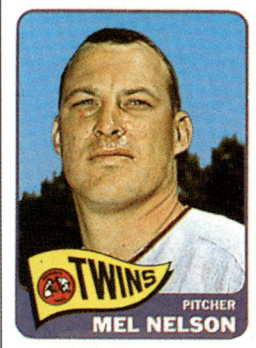

PITCHER
MEL NELSON

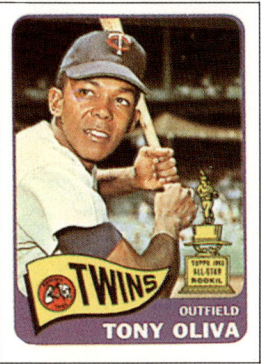

OUTFIELD
TONY OLIVA

PITCHER
CAMILO PASCUAL

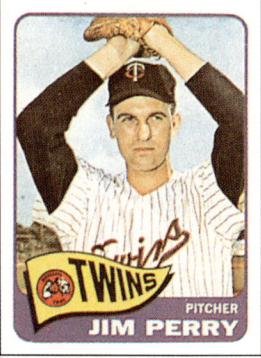

PITCHER
JIM PERRY

PITCHER
BILL PLEIS

CATCHER
KEN RETZER

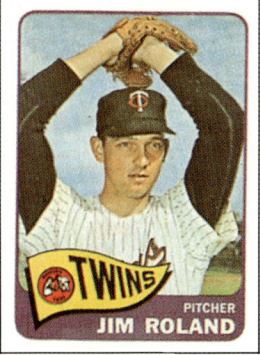

PITCHER
JIM ROLAND

TWINS 3rd BASE RICH ROLLINS

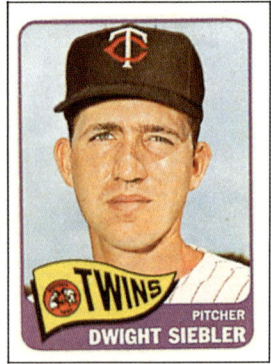

TWINS PITCHER DWIGHT SIEBLER

TWINS PITCHER DICK STIGMAN

TWINS SHORTSTOP ZOILO VERSALLES

TWINS PITCHER AL WORTHINGTON

TWINS CATCHER JERRY ZIMMERMAN

1965 ROOKIE STARS TWINS CESAR TOVAR infield SANDY VALDESPINO of

1965 ROOKIE STARS TWINS JAY WARD 3b-of GARY DOTTER pitcher

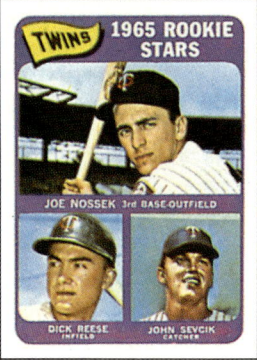

TWINS 1965 ROOKIE STARS JOE NOSSEK 3rd BASE-OUTFIELD DICK REESE INFIELD JOHN SEVCIK CATCHER

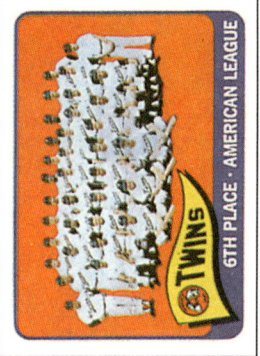

TWINS 6TH PLACE · AMERICAN LEAGUE

1966

Poised to repeat their championship, the Twins instead saw their run production drop and were unable to recover from a poor start, finishing second (89-73), 9 games behind Baltimore.

Only two Twins hit over .260, Tony Oliva (.307) and Harmon Killebrew (.281), as the club scored 111 fewer runs than during the previous year. After standing 8 games under .500 (35-43) on July 3 the club won 54 of its last 84 but still fell short. Killebrew was second in the league with 39 home runs and had a club-high 110 RBIs while Oliva had 25 homers and 87 RBIs but slumped badly (5-for-41) after hitting in the .320s into August.

Jim Kaat had an outstanding season with a 25-13 record, leading the league in wins, finishing sixth in ERA (2.74) and winning 8 straight games at one stage. Dave Boswell was 12-5 but didn't pitch after Aug. 7 owing to a shoulder injury. Jim (Mudcat) Grant slumped to 13-13. One highlight came on June 9 when five Twins homered in the seventh inning against Kansas City (Rich Rollins, Oliva, Zoilo Versalles, Killebrew and Don Mincher).

BERNIE ALLEN 2nd base

BOB ALLISON outfield

EARL BATTEY catcher

JIM GRANT pitcher

JIMMIE HALL outfield

JIM KAAT pitcher

HARMON KILLEBREW 3b-1b

JOHNNY KLIPPSTEIN pitcher

SAM MELE manager

JIM MERRITT pitcher

DON MINCHER 1st base

MEL NELSON pitcher

JOE NOSSEK of-3b

TONY OLIVA outfield

CAMILO PASCUAL pitcher

JIM PERRY pitcher

FRANK QUILICI 2b

GARRY ROGGENBURK pitcher

RICH ROLLINS infield

DWIGHT SIEBLER pitcher

SANDY VALDESPINO outfield

ZOILO VERSALLES shortstop

AL WORTHINGTON pitcher

JERRY ZIMMERMAN catcher

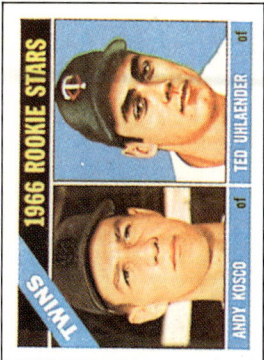

1967

Starting poorly for the second straight season, the Twins still managed to become involved in one of the most exciting pennant races in American League history. With a record of 25-25 on the morning of June 9, the Twins were sixth when manager Sam Mele was fired and replaced by Cal Ermer. Then the team won 12 of 15 to reach third place and moved into first on Aug. 13, touching off a three-cornered race with Detroit and Boston that lasted until the final day of the season. From that point, the Twins were never more than 1½ games behind nor more than 2 games in front of the rest of the league until losing the final two games of the year at Boston to finish second (91-71), tied with the Tigers, one game behind the Red Sox.

Harmon Killebrew tied for the league lead in homers (44) and had 113 RBIs while Tony Oliva hit .289 with 17 homers and 83 RBIs. Dean Chance who pitched two no-hitters in August, finished 20-14 and Jim Kaat was 16-13 but lost the season's final game.

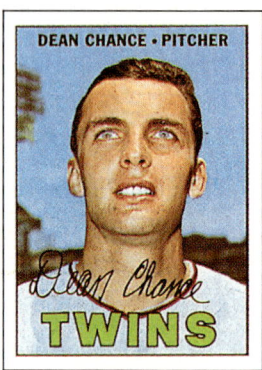

DEAN CHANCE · PITCHER
TWINS

JIM GRANT · PITCHER
TWINS

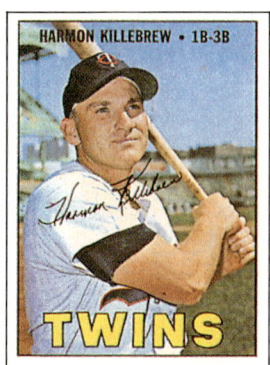

HARMON KILLEBREW · 1B-3B
TWINS

RON KLINE · PITCHER
TWINS

ANDY KOSCO · OUTFIELD
TWINS

SAM MELE · MGR
TWINS

JIM MERRITT · PITCHER
TWINS

RUSS NIXON · CATCHER
TWINS

TONY OLIVA OUTFIELD
TWINS

JIM PERRY · PITCHER
TWINS

RICH ROLLINS 3B-2B
TWINS

DWIGHT SIEBLER · P
TWINS

CESAR TOVAR · 2B
TWINS

TED UHLAENDER · OF
TWINS

ZOILO VERSALLES · SS
TWINS

AL WORTHINGTON · P
TWINS

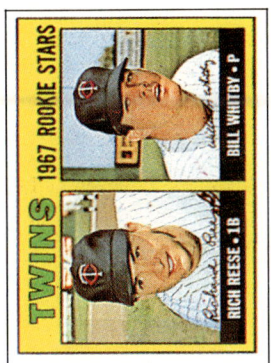

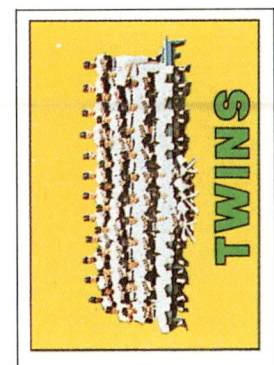

1968

Ready for another scramble for the pennant, the Twins and their fans were sorely disappointed. After winning the first 6 games of the season and taking first place, the club lost 12 of the next 20 to settle into seventh where it finished (79-83), 24 games out.

Injuries played a major role. Jim Kaat hurt his arm in the final game of the 1967 season and was unable to pitch until May, winning his first game on May 17. Harmon Killebrew pulled a hamstring in the All-Star Game and Tony Oliva separated his shoulder on Aug. 31 to end his season. Oliva hit .289 with 18 homers and 68 RBIs before being sidelined. Killebrew hit only .210 with 17 homers and 40 RBIs in 100 games. Ted Uhlaender (.283) and Cesar Tovar (.272) were among the leading hitters along with Rod Carew who hit .273 in his second season.

Dean Chance was 16-16 with a 2.53 ERA while Kaat finished at 14-12. Jim Merritt was 12-16, Dave Boswell 10-13 and Jim Perry 8-6.

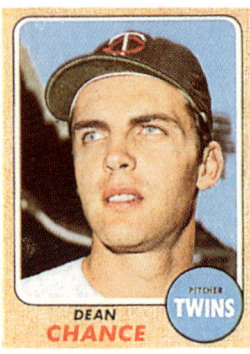

DEAN
CHANCE
PITCHER TWINS

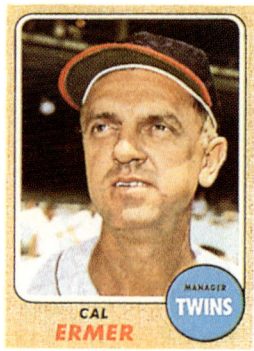

CAL
ERMER
MANAGER TWINS

JACKIE
HERNANDEZ
SHORTSTOP TWINS

JIM
KAAT
PITCHER TWINS

HARMON
KILLEBREW
1st BASE TWINS

The Sporting News
ALL STAR
SELECTION
68
HARMON KILLEBREW
FIRST BASE
AMERICAN LEAGUE

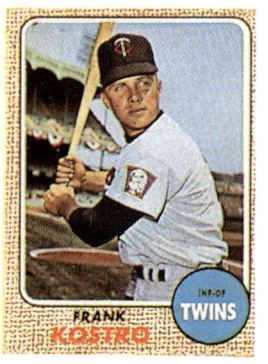

FRANK
KOSTRO
INF-OF TWINS

JIM
MERRITT
PITCHER TWINS

BOB
MILLER
PITCHER TWINS

RUSS
NIXON
CATCHER TWINS

TONY
OLIVA
OUTFIELD TWINS

The Sporting News
ALL STAR
SELECTION
68
TONY OLIVA
OUTFIELDER
AMERICAN LEAGUE

JIM
OLLOM
PITCHER TWINS

RON
PERRANOSKI
PITCHER TWINS

JIM
PERRY
PITCHER TWINS

FRANK
QUILICI
2B-SS TWINS

RICH
REESE

JIM
ROLAND

RICH
ROLLINS

CESAR
TOVAR

TED
UHLAENDER

AL
WORTHINGTON

JERRY
ZIMMERMAN

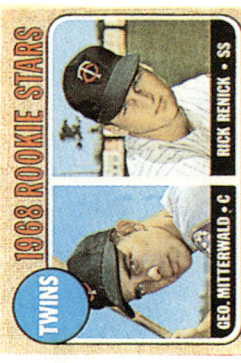

1968 ROOKIE STARS
RICK RENICK • SS
GEO. MITTERWALD • C
TWINS

1968 ROOKIE STARS
MOE OGIER • P
RON CLARK • 3B
TWINS

TWINS
AMERICAN LEAGUE

1969

With Cal Ermer fired on the day after the 1968 season ended, the Twins had Billy Martin as manager in 1969 and produced a surprise recovery to finish first in the new American League West. Regaining first place on July 5, the Twins solidified their hold with a blistering 23-7 July and finished 97-65, 9 games ahead. Unfortunately, in the first championship series, the Baltimore Orioles swept to the pennant in three games, 4-3, 1-0 and 11-2.

It was a season enlivened by such unusual events as Rod Carew stealing home 7 times to match a record and Martin punching pitcher Dave Boswell. Harmon Killebrew led the majors in homers (49) and RBIs (140) while hitting .276. Tony Oliva hit .309, Rich Reese .322 and Cesar Tovar .288 but Carew was the star, leading the league with a .332 average. For the first time, the Twins had two 20-game winners in Boswell (20-12) and Jim Perry (20-6). Jim Kaat was 14-13 and Ron Perranoski set a record with 31 saves.

  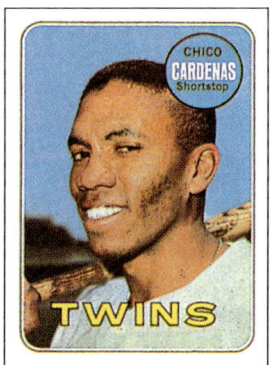 

 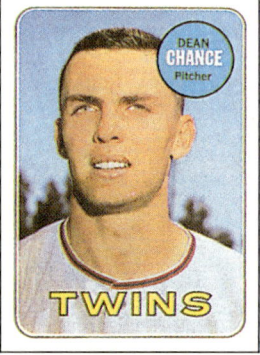  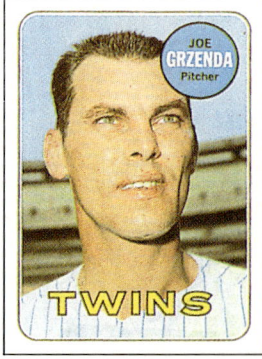

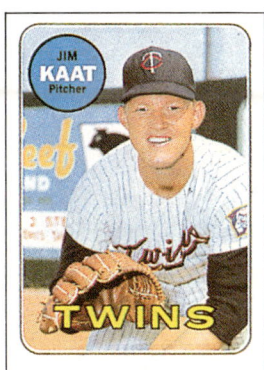

JIM KAAT
Pitcher
TWINS

HARMON KILLEBREW
3B-1B
TWINS

FRANK KOSTRO
INF-OF
TWINS

BRUCE LOOK
Catcher
TWINS

BILLY MARTIN
Manager
TWINS

BOB MILLER
Pitcher
TWINS

The Sporting News
TONY OLIVA
Outfield
TWINS
AMERICAN LEAGUE ALL-STARS

TONY OLIVA
Outfield
TWINS

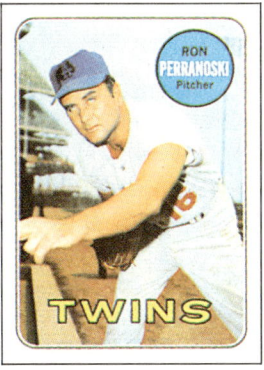

RON PERRANOSKI
Pitcher
TWINS

JIM PERRY
Pitcher
TWINS

FRANK QUILICI
Infield
TWINS

RICH REESE
1st Base
TWINS

JIM ROLAND
Pitcher
TWINS

JOHN ROSEBORO
Catcher
TWINS

CESAR TOVAR
3B-OF
TWINS

TED UHLAENDER
Outfield
TWINS

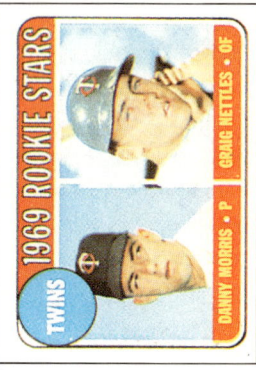 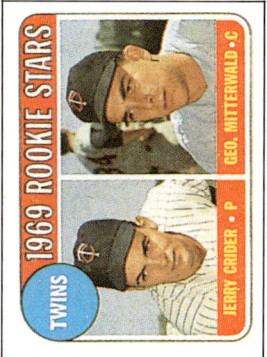

1970

Despite winning the division, Billy Martin was not rehired as the manager and the Twins started spring training with a new pilot for third straight year as Bill Rigney took the reins. Producing an even better record (98-64), the Twins repeated the division title to finish 9 games ahead again. But, once more, Baltimore won the playoffs in three straight games, 10-6, 11-3 and 6-1.

Leading the league in hitting, the Twins were paced by Tony Oliva (.325) and Cesar Tovar (.300). Harmon Killebrew hit 41 home runs and had 113 RBIs. Oliva hit 23 homers and drove in 107 runs.

Jim Perry won the Cy Young Award for his 20-12 season and 3.03 ERA that included 40 starts and 13 complete games. Rookie Bert Blyleven was 10-9, Jim Kaat was 14-10 and lefthander Tom Hall 11-6 with a 2.55 ERA. In relief the Twins had Ron Perranoski (7-8) with a record 34 saves and Al Williams (10-1) who had a 1.99 ERA and 15 saves.

Bob Allison | OUTFIELD Dave Boswell | PITCHER Leo Cardenas | SHORTSTOP Rod Carew | 2ND BASE

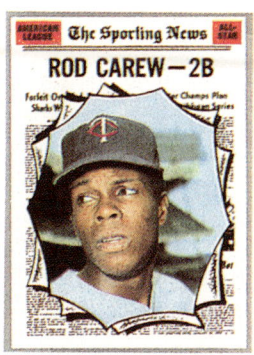

The Sporting News ALL-STAR
ROD CAREW—2B

TWINS

Tom Hall | PITCHER

TWINS

Jim Kaat | PITCHER

TWINS

Harmon Killebrew | 3B-1B

TWINS

Chuck Manuel | OUTFIELD

TWINS

Bob Miller | PITCHER

TWINS

George Mitterwald | CATCHER

TWINS

Tony Oliva | OUTFIELD

TWINS

Ron Perranoski | PITCHER

TWINS

Jim Perry | PITCHER

TWINS

Frank Quilici | 2ND BASE

TWINS

Rich Reese | 1ST BASE

TWINS

Rick Renick | 3B-SS

TWINS

Bill Rigney | MANAGER

TWINS

Luis Tiant | PITCHER

TWINS

Tom Tischinski | CATCHER

≡1971≡

By virtue of losing 10 of 12 during the season to the Baltimore Orioles and 12 of 18 to California, the Twins sank to fifth (74-86) and saw their attendance sink too. After ten straight seasons of more than one million paid admissions, the team drew only 940,858 to Metropolitan Stadium.

Tony Oliva won his third batting title with a .337 average, hitting 22 home runs and driving in 81 runs. Rod Carew hit .307 and Cesar Tovar .311. Harmon Killebrew provided a headline on Aug. 10 at the Met when he hit his 500th career home run off Mike Cuellar of Baltimore. It was the first of two he hit that day and he finished with a .254 average, 28 home runs (515 for his career) and led the league with 119 RBIs.

Jim Perry had a 17-17 record in spite of a 4.23 ERA, Bert Blyleven was 16-15 with a 2.82 ERA and Jim Kaat 13-14. One of the major failings was in the bullpen where Ray Corbin was the best (8-3) but Ron Perranoski did badly and was sold to Detroit on July 30.

TWINS
brant alyea • outfield

TWINS
bert blyleven • pitcher

TWINS
dave boswell • pitcher

TWINS
sal campisi • pitcher

TWINS
leo cardenas • shortstop

TWINS
rod carew • 2nd base

TWINS
tom hall • pitcher

TWINS
jim holt • outfield

TWINS
jim kaat • pitcher

TWINS
harmon killebrew • 1b

TWINS
chuck manuel • outfield

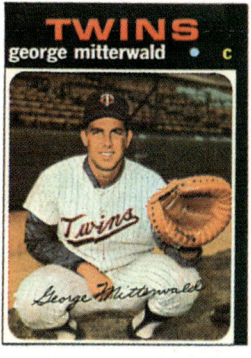

TWINS
george mitterwald • c

TWINS
tony oliva • outfield

TWINS
ron perranoski • pitcher

TWINS
jim perry • pitcher

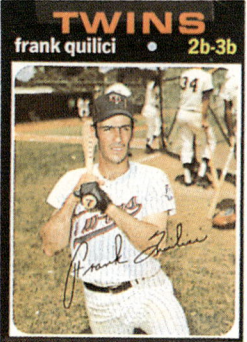

TWINS
frank quilici • 2b-3b

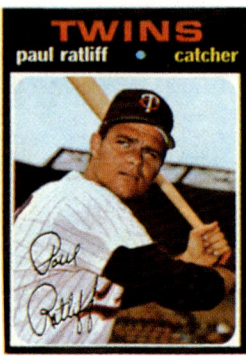

TWINS paul ratliff • catcher

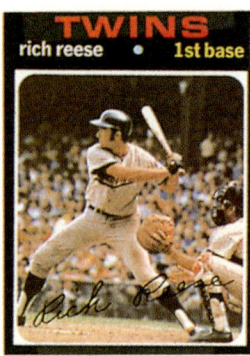

TWINS rich reese • 1st base

TWINS rick renick • 3rd base

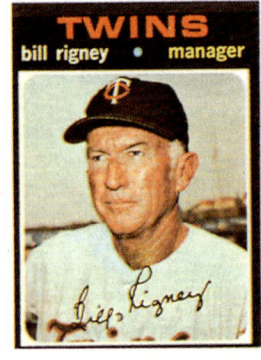

TWINS bill rigney • manager

TWINS danny thompson • 2b-ss

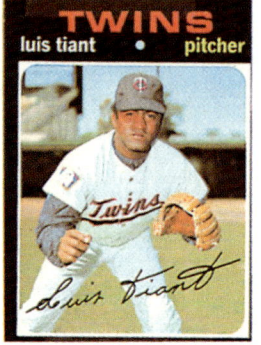

TWINS luis tiant • pitcher

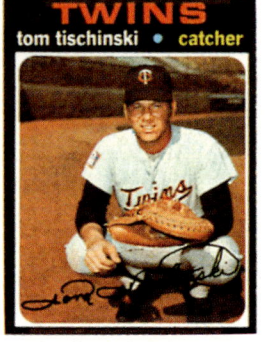

TWINS tom tischinski • catcher

TWINS cesar tovar • outfield

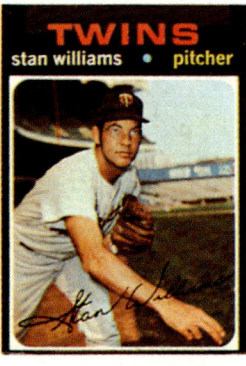

TWINS stan williams • pitcher

TWINS dick woodson • pitcher

TWINS bill zepp • pitcher

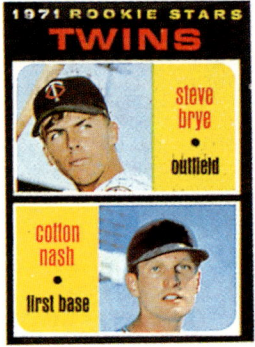

1971 ROOKIE STARS
TWINS
steve brye • outfield
cotton nash • first base

1971 ROOKIE STARS
TWINS
pete hamm • pitcher
jim nettles • outfield

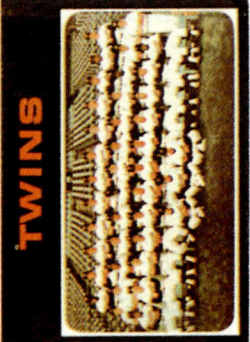

TWINS

1972

A players' strike delayed the start of the season for 10 days and when it started the Twins did well, winning 16 of the first 21, but then began to skid. On July 6 Bill Rigney was fired as manager with the team 36-34. Frank Quilici, at 33 the youngest manager in the majors, did slightly worse (41-43) and the club finished third with a 77-77 record, 15½ games out.

Rod Carew succeeded teammate Tony Oliva as the batting champion, hitting .318. Steve Braun hit .289 and young shortstop Danny Thompson .276. Harmon Killebrew led the club with 26 home runs, raising his career total to 541, the fourth best in history. Bobby Darwin (.267) hit 22 homers and had a club-high 80 RBIs but also set a club record with 145 strikeouts. Jim Kaat was 10-2 when he broke his hand on July 2 and didn't pitch again. Jim Perry (13-16) became the league's winningest active pitcher (180 wins). Bert Blyleven was 17-17 and Dick Woodson 14-14.

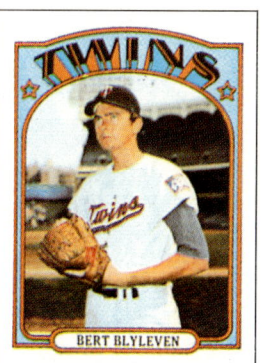
BERT BLYLEVEN

STEVE BRAUN

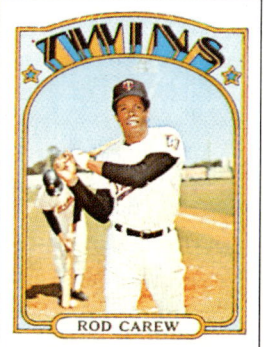
ROD CAREW

ROD CAREW IN ACTION

RAY CORBIN

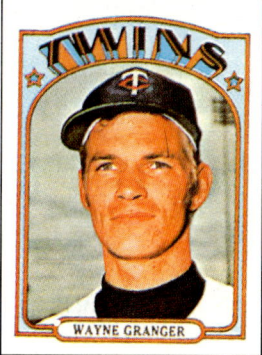
WAYNE GRANGER

PETE HAMM

JIM HOLT

JIM KAAT

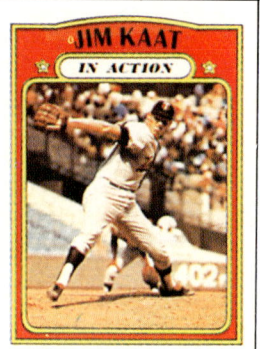

JIM KAAT
IN ACTION

HARMON KILLEBREW

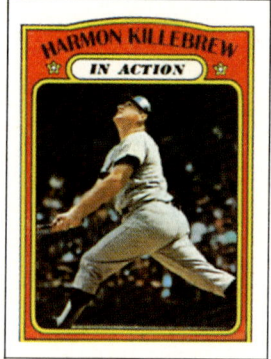

HARMON KILLEBREW
IN ACTION

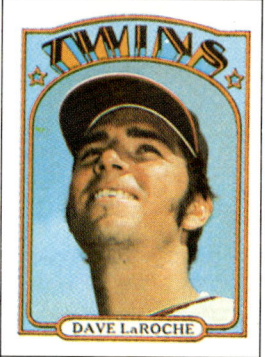

DAVE LaROCHE

STEVE LUEBBER

GEORGE MITTERWALD

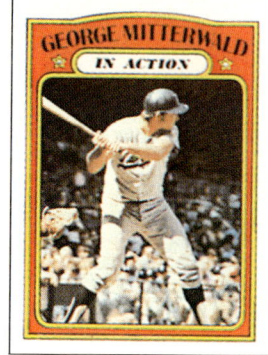

GEORGE MITTERWALD
IN ACTION

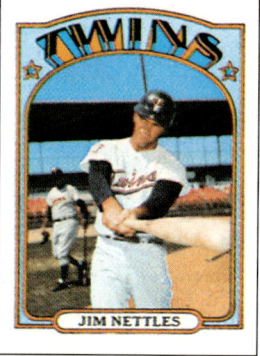

JIM NETTLES

TONY OLIVA

JIM PERRY

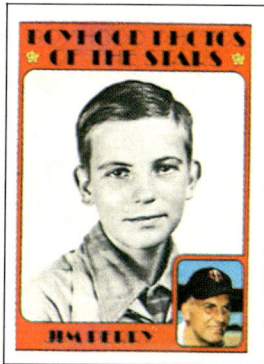

BOYHOOD PHOTOS
OF THE STARS

JIM PERRY

RICH REESE

RICK RENICK

BILL RIGNEY

PHIL ROOF

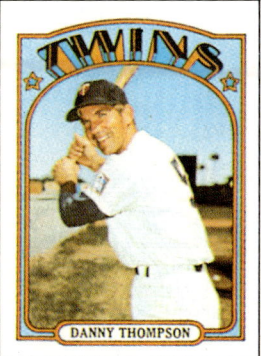

DANNY THOMPSON

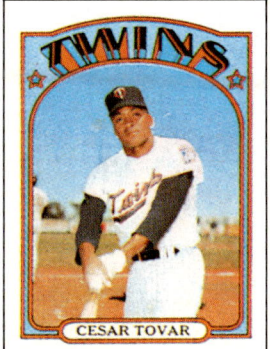

CESAR TOVAR

DICK WOODSON

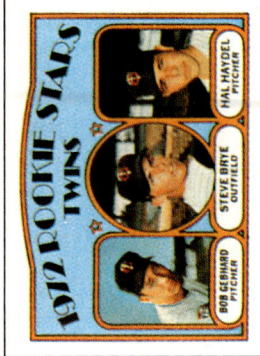

1972 ROOKIE STARS TWINS — HAL HAYDEL PITCHER / STEVE BRYE OUTFIELD / BOB GEBHARD PITCHER

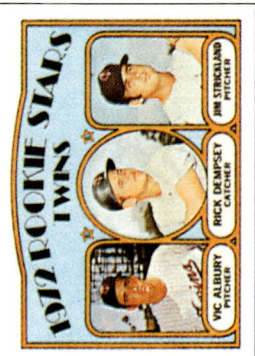

1972 ROOKIE STARS TWINS — JIM STRICKLAND PITCHER / RICK DEMPSEY CATCHER / VIC ALBURY PITCHER

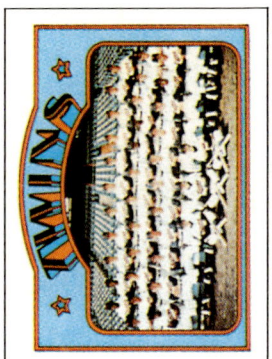

TWINS

1973

Thanks to the introduction of the designated hitter, the Twins were able to salvage the services of Tony Oliva, hobbled as he was by injuries. But even that help didn't move the Twins out of third place or above .500. They finished 81-81, 13 games out. Rod Carew won his third batting crown and second in a row with a .350 average, Oliva hit .291 with 16 homers and 92 RBIs. Jim Holt batted .297 and Steve Braun .283.

Bert Blyleven was 20-17 and set five team records, featuring a 2.52 ERA, second best in the league. He threw 25 complete games, pitched 325 innings, hurled 9 shutouts and struck out 258. Jim Kaat was 11-12 before being sold to the White Sox on Aug. 15. Dick Woodson had an arm injury and was only 10-8 while Joe Decker was 10-10. Ray Corbin was 8-5 (but 4-0 as a starter) and was joined in the bullpen by rookie Bill Campbell (3-3) who had 3 saves. Harmon Killebrew, slowed by injuries, had only 5 homers in 69 games.

BERT
BLYLEVEN
MINNESOTA TWINS
PITCHER

GLENN
BORGMANN
MINNESOTA TWINS
CATCHER

STEVE
BRAUN
MINNESOTA TWINS
3rd BASE

STEVE
BRYE
MINNESOTA TWINS
OUTFIELD

ROD
CAREW
MINNESOTA TWINS
2nd BASE

RAY
CORBIN
MINNESOTA TWINS
PITCHER

BOBBY
DARWIN
MINNESOTA TWINS
OUTFIELD

JOE
DECKER
MINNESOTA TWINS
PITCHER

DAVE
GOLTZ
MINNESOTA TWINS
PITCHER

BILL
HANDS
MINNESOTA TWINS
PITCHER

LARRY
HISLE
MINNESOTA TWINS
OUTFIELD

JIM
HOLT
MINNESOTA TWINS
OUTFIELD

JIM
KAAT
MINNESOTA TWINS
PITCHER

HARMON
KILLEBREW
MINNESOTA TWINS
1st BASE

DAN
MONZON
MINNESOTA TWINS
2nd BASE

JIM
NETTLES
MINNESOTA TWINS
OUTFIELD

TONY
OLIVA
MINNSEOTA TWINS
OUTFIELD

JIM
PERRY
MINNESOTA TWINS
PITCHER

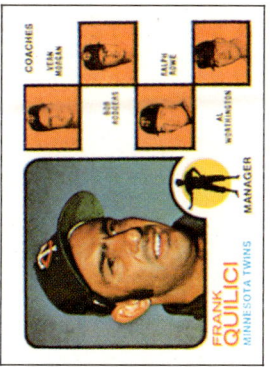

COACHES
VERN
MORGAN
RALPH
ROWE
BOB
RODGERS
AL
WORTHINGTON
FRANK
QUILICI
MINNESOTA TWINS
MANAGER

KEN
REYNOLDS
MINNESOTA TWINS
PITCHER

PHIL
ROOF
MINNESOTA TWINS
CATCHER

ERIC
SODERHOLM
MINNESOTA TWINS
3rd BASE

JIM
STRICKLAND
MINNESOTA TWINS
PITCHER

DANNY
THOMPSON
MINNESOTA TWINS
SHORTSTOP

DANNY
WALTON
MINNESOTA TWINS
OUTFIELD

DICK
WOODSON
MINNESOTA TWINS
PITCHER

MINNESOTA TWINS

1974

With Tony Oliva and Harmon Killebrew sharing the designated-hitter duties, the Twins season looked much like its predecessor. Improving one game (82-80), the team finished third for the third straight season, this time 8 games out.

Oliva hit .285 as a part-time player, slamming 13 homers with 57 RBIs. Killebrew (.222) had 13 homers to raise his career tally to 559 and drove in 54 runs but was released at the end of the season, signing with Kansas City. Bobby Darwin (.264) had 25 homers and 94 RBIs while Larry Hisle (.286) hit 19 homers with 79 RBIs. Rod Carew again won the batting title (.364), his third straight and fourth overall.

Bert Blyleven (17-17) had a 2.66 ERA with 249 strikeouts and 19 complete games. Joe Decker was 16-14 and Dave Goltz 10-10 but Bill Campbell became an outstanding reliever with an 8-7 record, a 2.63 ERA and 19 saves.

MINNESOTA PITCHER — RAY CORBIN — TWINS

MINNESOTA OUTFIELD — BOBBY DARWIN — TWINS

MINNESOTA PITCHER — JOE DECKER — TWINS

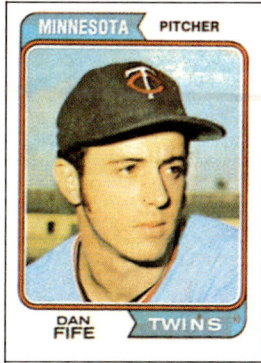

MINNESOTA PITCHER — DAN FIFE — TWINS

MINNESOTA PITCHER — DAVE GOLTZ — TWINS

MINNESOTA PITCHER — BILL HANDS — TWINS

MINNESOTA OUTFIELD — LARRY HISLE — TWINS

MINNESOTA OUTFIELD — JIM HOLT — TWINS

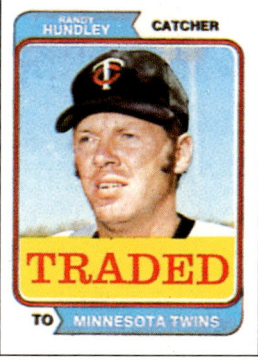

RANDY HUNDLEY CATCHER — TRADED TO MINNESOTA TWINS

MINNESOTA 1st BASE-DH — HARMON KILLEBREW — TWINS

MINNESOTA 1st BASE — JOE LIS — TWINS

MINNESOTA CATCHER — GEORGE MITTERWALD — TWINS

MINNESOTA INFIELD — DAN MONZON — TWINS

MINNESOTA DES. HITTER — TONY OLIVA — TWINS

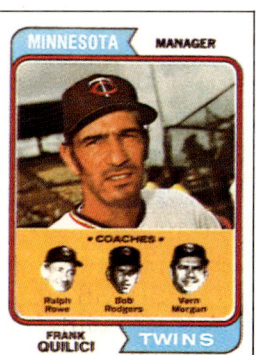

MINNESOTA MANAGER — COACHES — Ralph Rowe, Bob Rodgers, Vern Morgan — FRANK QUILICI — TWINS

MINNESOTA CATCHER — PHIL ROOF — TWINS

1975

This was the season in which Minnesota's fate was not determined until the final day, when the Twins failed to make it to third, slipping instead to fourth (76-83). Manager Frank Quilici was told before the finale that he would not be brought back but did not tell his players, hoping they would win the last game to hold third. But the Twins lost, 6-4, in 10 innings to Chicago while Texas won, 3-1, over Kansas City. Quilici had a 280-287 career managerial record.

Rod Carew's fifth batting title, his fourth straight, came on a .359 average with 14 homers and 80 RBIs. He became the first hitter since the legendary Ty Cobb to win more than three batting crowns in a row. Cobb won 9 straight from 1907 to 1915. Larry Hisle hit .314, Steve Braun and Phil Roof .302 and Tony Oliva .270 with 13 homers and 58 RBIs. Two rookies, Lyman Bostock (.282) and Dan Ford (.280 with 15 homers), added some punch to the lineup.

Bert Blyleven was 15-10 with a 3.00 ERA and 20 complete games while Jim Hughes (16-14) was the winningest rookie in the major leagues.

TWINS
VIC ALBURY — Pitcher

TWINS
BERT BLYLEVEN — Pitcher

TWINS
GLENN BORGMANN — Catcher

TWINS
STEVE BRAUN — Outfield

TWINS
STEVE BRYE — Outfield

TWINS
TOM BURGMEIER — Pitcher

TWINS
BILL BUTLER — Pitcher

TWINS
BILL CAMPBELL — Pitcher

TWINS
ROD CAREW — AL ALL STAR 2nd Base

TWINS
RAY CORBIN — Pitcher

TWINS
BOBBY DARWIN — Outfield

TWINS
JOE DECKER — Pitcher

TWINS
DAVE GOLTZ — Pitcher

TWINS
LARRY HISLE — Outfield

TWINS
HARMON KILLEBREW — DH-1B

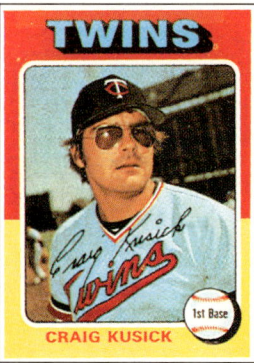
TWINS
CRAIG KUSICK — 1st Base

TONY OLIVA

PHIL ROOF

ERIC SODERHOLM

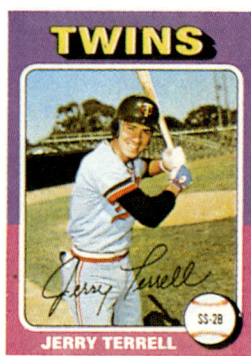
JERRY TERRELL

DANNY THOMPSON

1976

Gene Mauch made his Minnesota managerial debut with a team that returned to third place (85-77) and was just 5 games out of first. On June 1 he lost his most reliable pitcher when Bert Blyleven was traded to Texas along with shortstop Danny Thompson for four players and $250,000.

Rod Carew hit .331 but did not win the batting title, losing a torrid three-way tussle with Kansas City's George Brett (.333) and Hal McRae (.332). Lyman Bostock (.323) finished fourth in the batting race. Carew had a strong all-round year, driving in 90 runs and setting a club record with 49 stolen bases. Larry Hisle (.272) hit 14 homers and led the club with 96 RBIs and Dan Ford (.260) had a club-best 20 homers as well as 86 RBIs.

Bill Campbell was 17-5 in a team-record 78 games, posting 20 saves, and then signed with Boston as a free agent after the season. Bill Singer, obtained from Texas for Blyleven, was 9-9 and Dave Goltz 14-14.

VIC ALBURY
PITCHER
TWINS

BERT BLYLEVEN
PITCHER
TWINS

GLENN BORGMANN
CATCHER
TWINS

LYMAN BOSTOCK
OUTFIELD
TWINS

STEVE BRAUN
OUTFIELD
TWINS

JOHNNY BRIGGS
OUTFIELD
TWINS

STEVE BRYE
TWINS

TOM BURGMEIER
PITCHER
TWINS

BILL BUTLER
TWINS

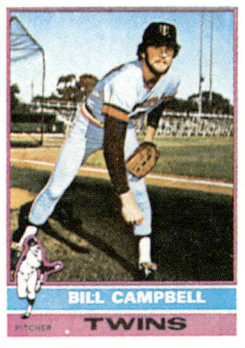

BILL CAMPBELL
PITCHER
TWINS

AL ALL STAR 2nd Base
ROD CAREW
TWINS

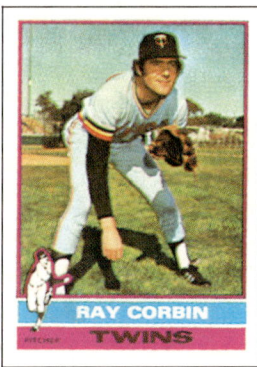

RAY CORBIN
PITCHER
TWINS

JOE DECKER
TWINS

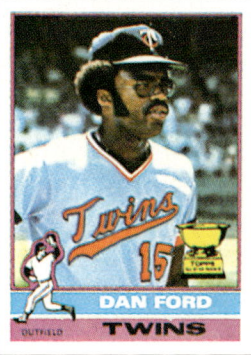

DAN FORD
OUTFIELD
TWINS

DAVE GOLTZ
PITCHER
TWINS

LARRY HISLE
OUTFIELD
TWINS

JIM HUGHES
TWINS

TOM JOHNSON
TWINS

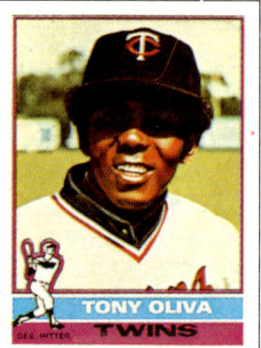
TONY OLIVA
TWINS

PHIL ROOF
TWINS

ERIC SODERHOLM
TWINS

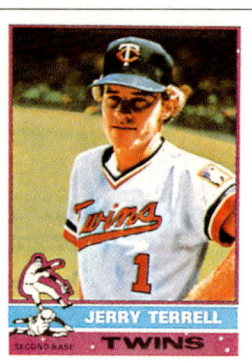
JERRY TERRELL
TWINS

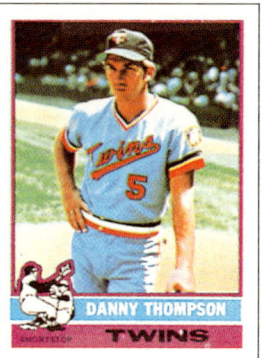
DANNY THOMPSON
TWINS

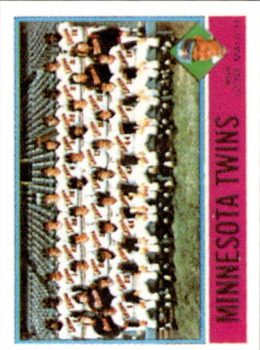
MINNESOTA TWINS

≡1977≡

A team seemingly destined to finish higher instead lost 18 of its last 27 and staggered home fourth (84-77), 17 ½ games behind. Rod Carew, in his finest season, hit .388 with 14 home runs and 100 RBIs, winning the batting title for the sixth time and also leading the league in runs scored (128) and triples (16). Lyman Bostock was the runner-up in batting (.336) with 14 homers and 90 RBIs while Larry Hisle hit .302 with a club high in homers (28) and led the league with 119 RBIs.

Despite setting a club record for runs scored (867), the offense failed to offset the pitching problems. Two young hurlers, Mike Pazik and Dan Carrithers, were severely injured in an auto crash April 25 that finished Pazik for the season. Carrithers returned in August from a sprained knee and broken wrist but was ineffective. Dave Goltz was 20-11 with 19 complete games and Tommy Johnson 16-7 with 15 saves but things got so bad that major league pitching coach Jim Shellenback was added to the roster in September along with 20-year-old Gary Serum.

TWINS — PITCHER — VIC ALBURY

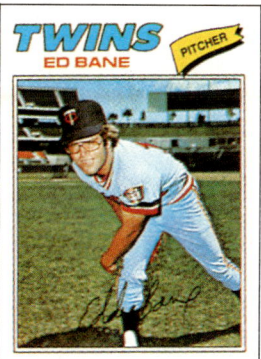
TWINS — PITCHER — ED BANE

TWINS — CATCHER — GLENN BORGMANN

TWINS — OUTFIELD — LYMAN BOSTOCK

TWINS — OUTFIELD — STEVE BRYE

TWINS — PITCHER — TOM BURGMEIER

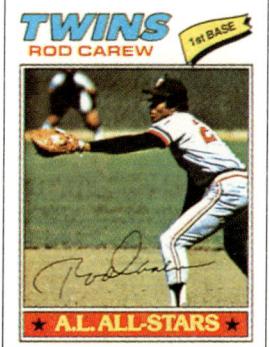
TWINS — 1st BASE — ROD CAREW
A.L. ALL-STARS ★

TWINS — 3rd BASE — MIKE CUBBAGE

TWINS — OUTFIELD — DAN FORD

TWINS — PITCHER — DAVE GOLTZ

TWINS — SHORTSTOP — LUIS GOMEZ

TWINS — OUTFIELD — LARRY HISLE

TWINS — PITCHER — JIM HUGHES

TWINS — PITCHER — TOM JOHNSON

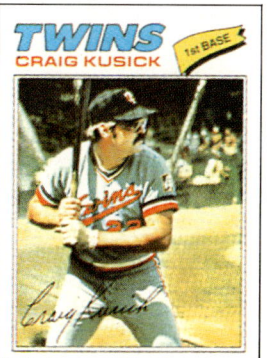
TWINS — 1st BASE — CRAIG KUSICK

TWINS — PITCHER — STEVE LUEBBER

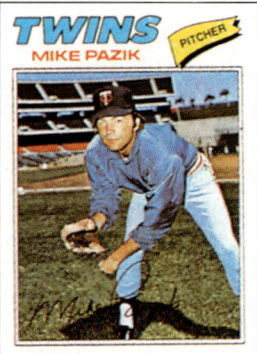

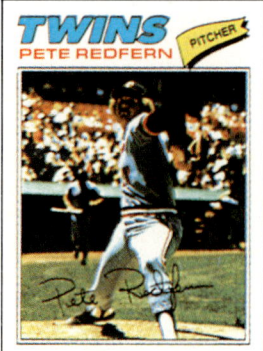

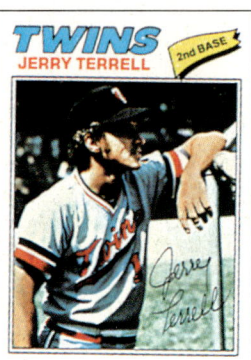

1978

Hit by the loss of two of their most promising players, Lyman Bostock (to California) and Larry Hisle (to Milwaukee) in the free agent draft, the Twins muddled home fourth (73-89), 19 games back. Rod Carew collected his second batting title in a row and seventh overall (in 10 seasons) with a .333 average but he had little support. Shortstop Roy Smalley (.272) led the team in homers (19) and had 77 RBIs. Dan Ford (.274) had 11 homers and a team-high 82 RBIs while third baseman Mike Cubbage hit .282. Cubbage, like Smalley, had been obtained in the trade with Texas for pitcher Bert Blyleven the year before.

But pitching remained a constant problem as the Twins started with an 8-16 April and had only one winning month (15-13 in September). Dave Goltz (15-10) was injured and started only 29 games. Manager Gene Mauch persuaded owner Calvin Griffith to sign free agent Mike Marshall on May 15 and Marshall was 10-12 with a 2.45 ERA and 21 saves in 54 games. Geoff Zahn was 14-14 and Roger Erickson 14-13.

GLENN ADAMS

GLENN BORGMANN

TERRY BULLING

TOM BURGMEIER

ROD CAREW

DON CARRITHERS

RICH CHILES

MIKE CUBBAGE

DAN FORD

DAVE GOLTZ

BOB GORINSKI

DAVE JOHNSON

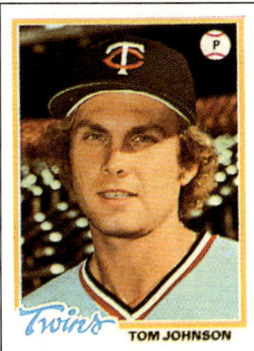

TOM JOHNSON

CRAIG KUSICK

GENE MAUCH

BOB RANDALL

PETE REDFERN

BOMBO RIVERA

ROY SMALLEY

PAUL THORMODSGARD

BUTCH WYNEGAR

GEOFF ZAHN

1979

On Feb. 3 the Twins made the momentous move of trading seven-times batting champion Rod Carew to California for outfielder Ken Landreaux, third baseman Dave Engel and pitchers Paul Hartzell and Brad Havens. Landreaux led the Twins in hitting with a .305 average and had 15 homers and 83 RBIs as the team finished fourth (82-80) again, but this time only 6 games back. Roy Smalley was the top power hitter with 24 homers and 95 RBIs but endured a terrific slump in July and August. He was batting .372 on July 4 but finished at .271.

Lefthander Jerry Koosman, obtained in an offseason deal with the Mets, produced a 20-13 season and a 3.38 ERA. Geoff Zahn was 13-7 and Dave Goltz was 14-13. Mike Marshall was the star of the bullpen with a 10-15 record, a 2.64 ERA, 32 saves and a record 90 appearances.

At the end of the season, the team announced a move to a domed stadium in downtown Minneapolis.

GLENN ADAMS OF
TWINS

GLENN BORGMANN C
TWINS

A.L. ALL★STAR
ROD CAREW 1B
TWINS

RICH CHILES DH
TWINS

MIKE CUBBAGE 3B
TWINS

ROGER ERICKSON P
TWINS

DAN FORD OF
TWINS

DAVE GOLTZ P
TWINS

JEFF HOLLY P
TWINS

DARRELL JACKSON P
TWINS

TOM JOHNSON P
TWINS

CRAIG KUSICK 1B-DH
TWINS

JOSE MORALES C-1B
TWINS

WILLIE NORWOOD OF
TWINS

HOSKEN POWELL OF
TWINS

BOB RANDALL 2B
TWINS

PETE REDFERN P

TWINS

BOMBO RIVERA OF

TWINS

GARY SERUM P

TWINS

ROY SMALLEY SS

TWINS

JOHNNY SUTTON P

TWINS

PAUL THORMODSGARD P

TWINS

ROB WILFONG 2B

TWINS

LARRY WOLFE 3B

TWINS

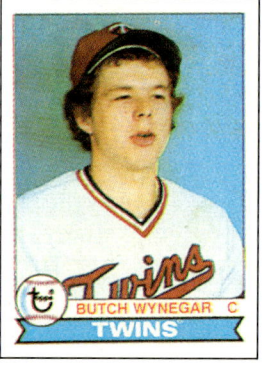

BUTCH WYNEGAR C

TWINS

GEOFF ZAHN P

TWINS

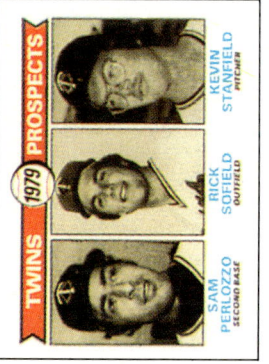

TWINS 1979 PROSPECTS

KEVIN STANFIELD PITCHER

RICK SOFIELD OUTFIELD

SAM PERLOZZO SECOND BASE

TWINS

GENE MAUCH MANAGER

1980

Another third-place finish, the resignation of manager Gene Mauch and the lowest attendance in the major leagues all came the Twins' way along with a 77-84 record. Mauch resigned on Aug. 24 after a 3-2 loss to Detroit with the team 54-71 and fourth, 26½ games out. Under John Groyl the club finished 23-13 to grab third. Minnesota won 19 of its last 25 including a 12-game winning streak, longest in the majors in two seasons.

No hitter finished in the league's top 15 but John Castino topped the club (.302) and also led the team in homers (13) and RBIs (64). Ken Landreaux hit .281 and his 31-game hitting streak was the best in the majors since Dom DiMaggio of Boston in 1949 hit in 34 straight.

Reliever Mike Marshall (1-3, 1 save) was released June 6 and claimed it was due to "union activities" but his formal grievance was not upheld. Jerry Koosman was 16-13 and Geoff Zahn, though only 14-18, pitched 5 shutouts.

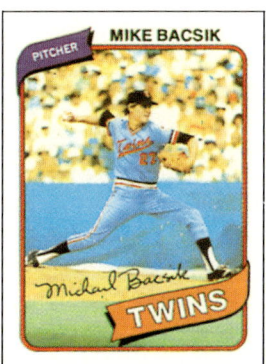
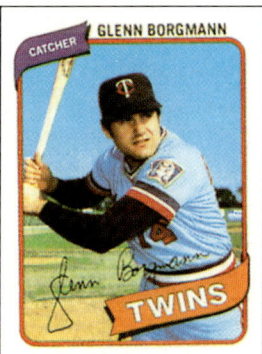
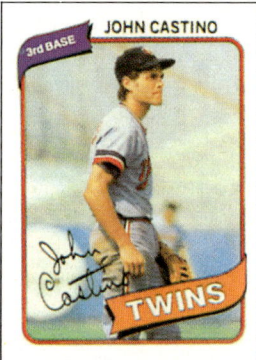

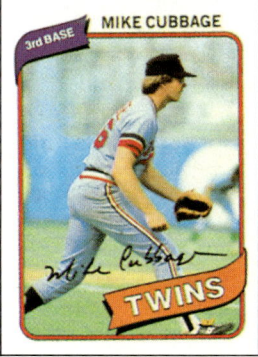
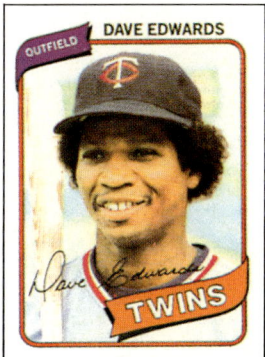

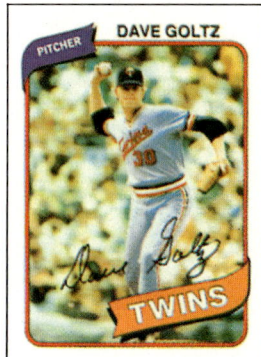

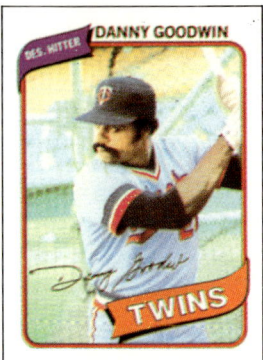

DES. HITTER — DANNY GOODWIN
TWINS

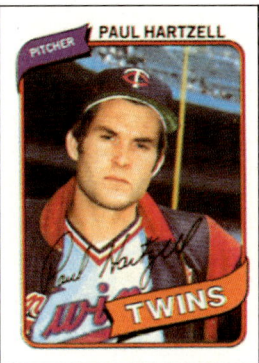

PITCHER — PAUL HARTZELL
TWINS

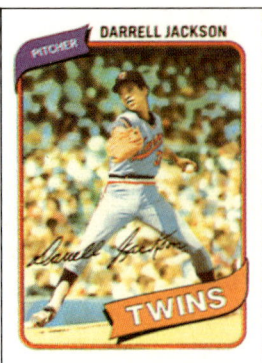

PITCHER — DARRELL JACKSON
TWINS

1st BASE — RON JACKSON
TWINS

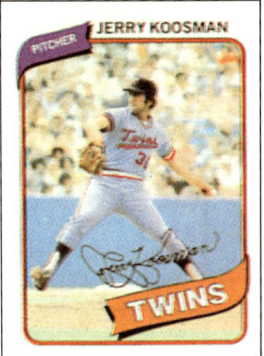

PITCHER — JERRY KOOSMAN
TWINS

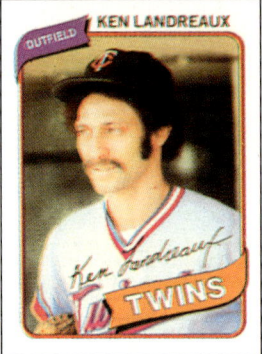

OUTFIELD — KEN LANDREAUX
TWINS

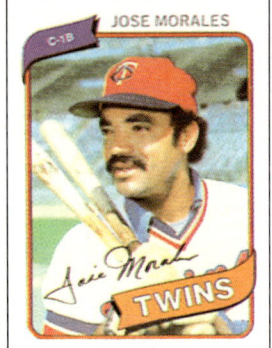

C-1B — JOSE MORALES
TWINS

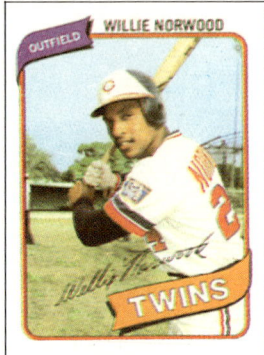

OUTFIELD — WILLIE NORWOOD
TWINS

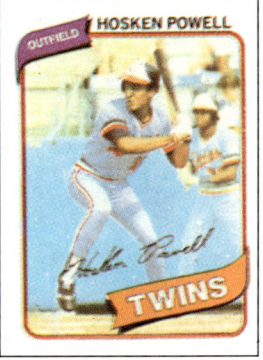

OUTFIELD — HOSKEN POWELL
TWINS

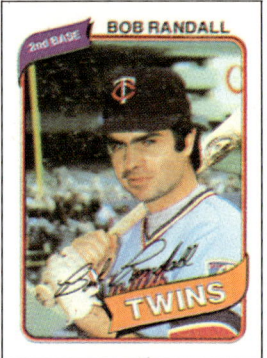

2nd BASE — BOB RANDALL
TWINS

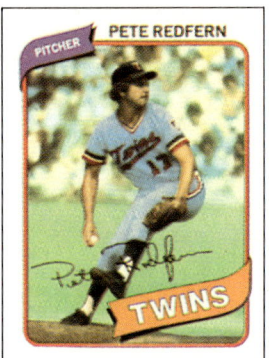

PITCHER — PETE REDFERN
TWINS

OUTFIELD — BOMBO RIVERA
TWINS

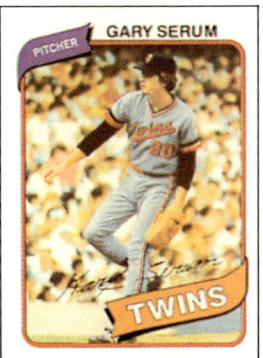

PITCHER — GARY SERUM
TWINS

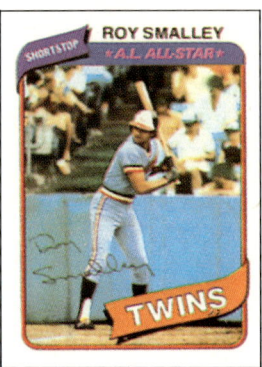

SHORTSTOP — ROY SMALLEY
★A.L. ALL-STAR★
TWINS

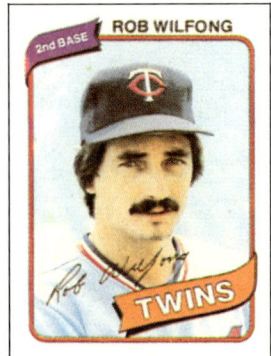

2nd BASE — ROB WILFONG
TWINS

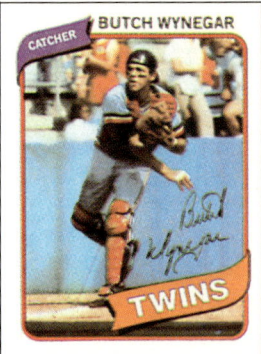

CATCHER — BUTCH WYNEGAR
TWINS

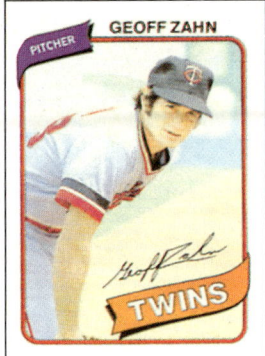

1981

In a season split in half by the players' strike, the Twins looked like two different teams. In the first half they were 17-39, a distant seventh. In the second half they finished fourth but were 24-29 and not eliminated from a chance to win until late September. In the final season at Metropolitan Stadium in Bloomington, the Twins had the worst attendance in the majors (469,090) and the worst since the move to Minnesota in 1961.

John Castino underwent a spinal fusion and Roy Smalley also experienced back problems that limited him to 56 games although he hit .263. Three rookies (Kent Hrbek, Gary Gaetti and Tim Laudner) all homered in their first game but all three had only 9 homers for the season. The Twins hit just 47 homers for the year.

Pete Redfern was the top winner with a 9-8 record, Fernando Arroyo was 7-10 and Al Williams 6-10. Ken Landreaux was traded to Los Angeles during spring training.

DOUG CORBETT — PITCHER TWINS

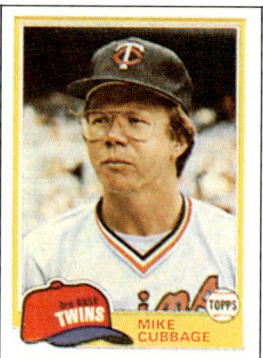
MIKE CUBBAGE — 3rd BASE TWINS

DAVE EDWARDS — OUTFIELD TWINS

ROGER ERICKSON — PITCHER TWINS

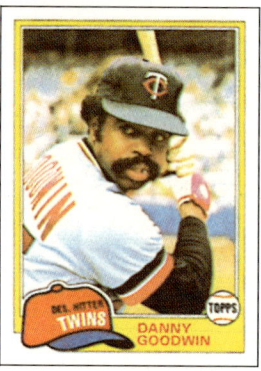
DANNY GOODWIN — DES. HITTER TWINS

MICKEY HATCHER — OUTFIELD TWINS

DARRELL JACKSON — PITCHER TWINS

RON JACKSON — 1st BASE TWINS

JERRY KOOSMAN — PITCHER TWINS

KEN LANDREAUX — OUTFIELD TWINS

PETE MACKANIN — 2nd BASE TWINS

JOSE MORALES — C-1B TWINS

HOSKEN POWELL — OUTFIELD TWINS

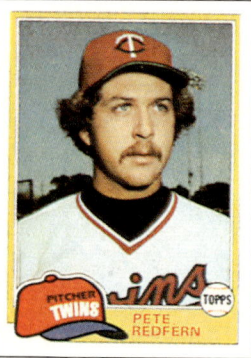
PETE REDFERN — PITCHER TWINS

BOMBO RIVERA — OUTFIELD TWINS

ROY SMALLEY — SHORTSTOP TWINS

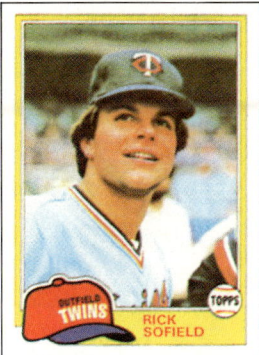

1982

Opening the first season in the new Humphrey Metrodome in downtown Minneapolis, the Twins staggered home seventh with the worst record (60-102) since the move to Minnesota. As a result, even the new stadium was not enough of an attraction as the Twins drew 921,186, the only team in the majors not to hit a million. Opening night (an 11-7 loss to Seattle) drew 52,279 but from May 30 through June 2 the team won only 7 of 48 games and sank deep into last place. Early-season trades disposed of many familiar faces including Roy Smalley, Ray Corbett, Roger Erickson, Butch Wynegar and Rob Wilfong. In May, the Twins were 3-26, the poorest month by a major league team since June 1916, when the old Philadelphia A's were 2-28.

Kent Hrbek emerged as a genuine hitter, batting .301 with 23 homers and 92 RBIs, while Gary Ward (.289) hit 28 homers and had 92 RBIs. Bobby Castillo (13-11) was the leading pitcher.

TWINS — OUTFIELD — GLENN ADAMS

TWINS — PITCHER — FERNANDO ARROYO

TWINS — SHORTSTOP — CHUCK BAKER

TWINS — OUTFIELD — TOM BRUNANSKY

TWINS — CATCHER — SAL BUTERA

TWINS — PITCHER — BOBBY CASTILLO

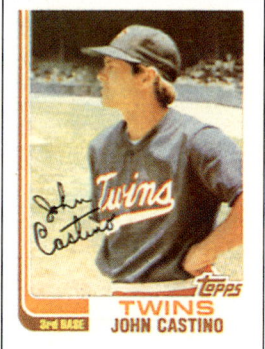

TWINS — 3rd BASE — JOHN CASTINO

TWINS — PITCHER — DON COOPER

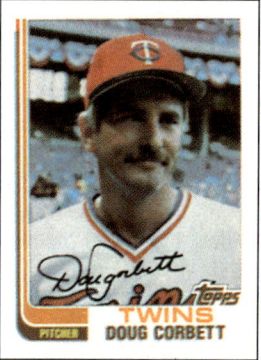

TWINS — PITCHER — DOUG CORBETT

TWINS — PITCHER — RON DAVIS

TWINS — OUTFIELD — DAVE ENGLE

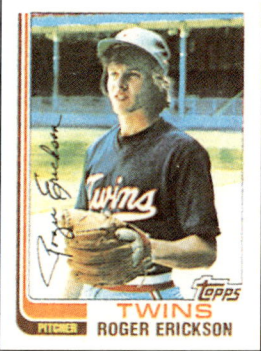

TWINS — PITCHER — ROGER ERICKSON

TWINS — DH — DANNY GOODWIN

TWINS — 3B-OF — MICKEY HATCHER

TWINS — PITCHER — BRAD HAVENS

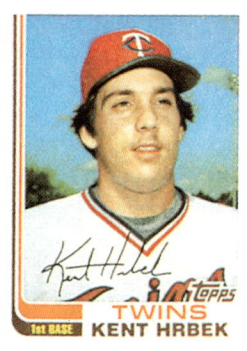

TWINS — 1st BASE — KENT HRBEK

TWINS
PITCHER DARRELL JACKSON

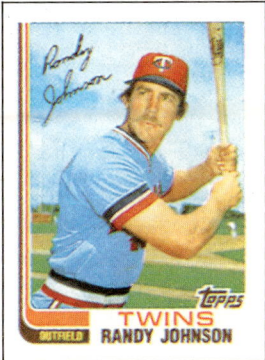

TWINS
OUTFIELD RANDY JOHNSON

TWINS
2nd BASE PETE MACKANIN

TWINS
PITCHER JACK O'CONNOR

TWINS
OUTFIELD HOSKEN POWELL

TWINS
PITCHER PETE REDFERN

TWINS
SHORTSTOP ROY SMALLEY

TWINS
OUTFIELD RICK SOFIELD

TWINS
PITCHER JOHN VERHOEVEN

TWINS
OUTFIELD GARY WARD

TWINS
SS-2B RON WASHINGTON

TWINS
2nd BASE ROB WILFONG

TWINS
PITCHER AL WILLIAMS

TWINS
CATCHER BUTCH WYNEGAR

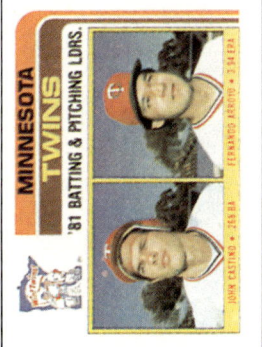

MINNESOTA
TWINS
'81 BATTING & PITCHING LDRS.

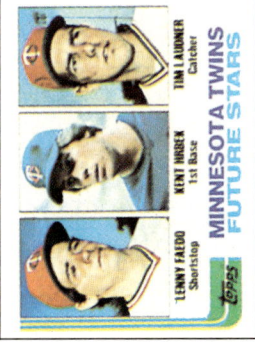

MINNESOTA TWINS
FUTURE STARS
TIM LAUDNER Catcher
KENT HRBEK 1st Base
LENNY FAEDO Shortstop

1983

Billy Gardner, who succeeded John Goryl in early 1981, started his second full season with hopes for improvement and the club moved up to a tie for fifth (70-92), gaining 10 games in its record.

Kent Hrbek batted .297 with 16 homers and 84 RBIs and Gary Ward (.278) had 19 homers and a team-high 88 RBIs. Shifted to catcher, Dave Engel hit .305 and Mickey Hatcher, whom the team tried to trade in the spring, hit .317 in 106 games. Gary Gaetti (.245) hit 21 homers and had 78 RBIs.

Ken Schrom was the top pitcher with a 15-8 record and Al Williams was 11-14. Bobby Castillo was 8-12 before being afflicted with a rotator-cuff injury in August. Ron Davis (5-8), who saved 22 games the previous season, increased to 30 saves and had a 3.34 ERA. Attendance dipped downward once more, to 858,939.

PAUL BORIS
PITCHER
TWINS

TOM BRUNANSKY
OUTFIELD
TWINS

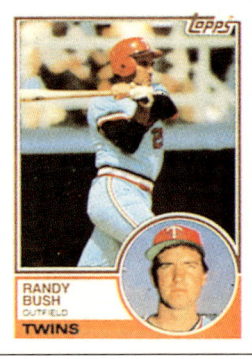
RANDY BUSH
OUTFIELD
TWINS

SAL BUTERA
CATCHER
TWINS

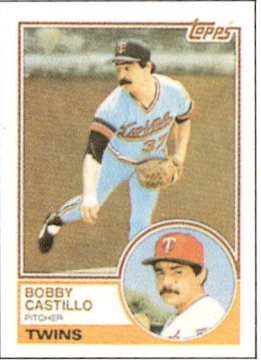
BOBBY CASTILLO
PITCHER
TWINS

JOHN CASTINO
3rd BASE-2nd BASE
TWINS

RON DAVIS
PITCHER
TWINS

JIM EISENREICH
OUTFIELD
TWINS

DAVE ENGLE
OUTFIELD
TWINS

LENNY FAEDO
SHORTSTOP
TWINS

TERRY FELTON
PITCHER
TWINS

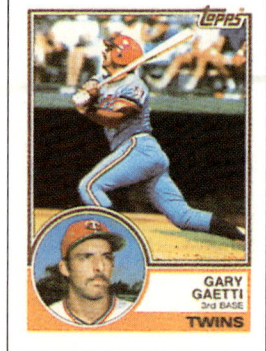

GARY GAETTI
3rd BASE
TWINS

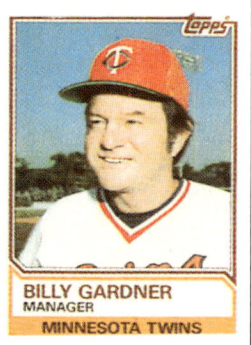

BILLY GARDNER
MANAGER
MINNESOTA TWINS

MICKEY HATCHER
3rd BASE-OUTFIELD
TWINS

BRAD HAVENS
PITCHER
TWINS

KENT HRBEK
1st BASE
TWINS

RANDY JOHNSON
OUTFIELD
TWINS

TIM LAUDNER
CATCHER
TWINS

JEFF LITTLE
PITCHER
TWINS

BOBBY MITCHELL
OUTFIELD
TWINS

JACK O'CONNOR
PITCHER
TWINS

JOHN PACELLA
PITCHER
TWINS

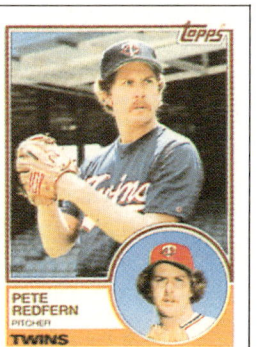

PETE REDFERN
PITCHER
TWINS

JESUS VEGA
1st BASE
TWINS

FRANK
VIOLA
PITCHER
TWINS

GARY
WARD
OUTFIELD
TWINS

RON
WASHINGTON
SS-3rd BASE
TWINS

LEN
WHITEHOUSE
PITCHER
TWINS

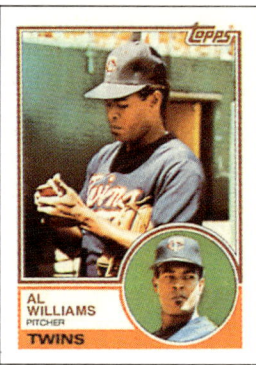
AL
WILLIAMS
PITCHER
TWINS

1982 BATTING & PITCHING LEADERS
BOBBY CASTILLO
3.66 ERA
KENT HRBEK
.301 BA
MINNESOTA TWINS

1984

On July 31 the sale of the team by Calvin Griffith and his sister Thelma Griffith Haynes was finalized. Over a month earlier, on June 22, an emotional ceremony had been held at home plate when 52 percent of the club was signed over to Carl Pohlad. The final sale price was $35 million. Perhaps in response, the Twins surged to the top of the standings and by Aug. 22 were in first place but then lost 11 of 14. They tied for first again in the final week but lost the last 6 games including a bizarre game at Cleveland where Minnesota had a 10-0 lead and lost, 11-10. It was the biggest lead ever lost by the Twins team. Minnesota finished second (81-81).

Kent Hrbek batted .311 with 27 homers and 107 RBIs, Mickey Hatcher hit .302 and Tom Brunansky (.254) led the club with 32 homers. He drove in 85 runs. Kirby Puckett hit .298.

An offseason trade brought pitchers Mike Smithson and John Butcher for Gary Ward. Smithson was 15-13 and Butcher 13-11 but Frank Viola was the leading pitcher with an 18-12 record and Ron Davis had 29 saves.

DARRELL BROWN OF

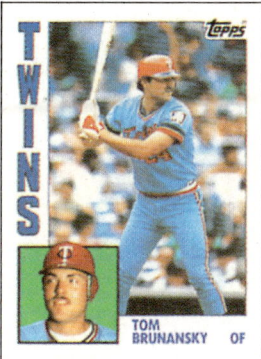

TOM BRUNANSKY OF

RANDY BUSH OF

JOHN BUTCHER P

BOBBY CASTILLO P

JOHN CASTINO 2B

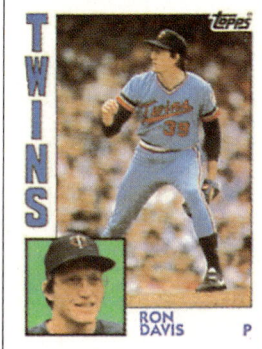

RON DAVIS P

DAVE ENGLE C

LENNY FAEDO SS

PETE FILSON P

GARY GAETTI 3B

MANAGER
BILLY GARDNER

MICKEY HATCHER 3B-OF

BRAD HAVENS P

KENT HRBEK 1B

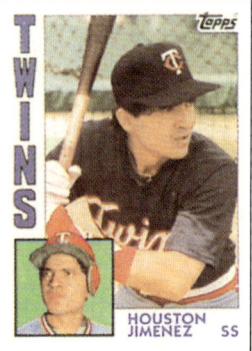

HOUSTON JIMENEZ SS

RUSTY KUNTZ OF

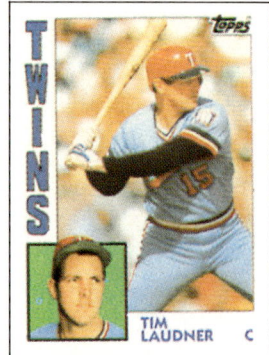

TIM LAUDNER C

RICK LYSANDER P

BOBBY MITCHELL OF

JACK O'CONNOR P

KEN SCHROM P

RAY SMITH C

MIKE SMITHSON P

TIM TEUFEL 2B

SCOTT ULLGER OF-1B

FRANK VIOLA P

MIKE WALTERS P

GARY WARD OF

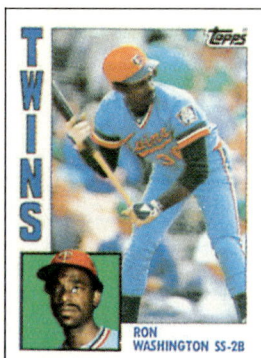

RON WASHINGTON SS-2B

LEN WHITEHOUSE

AL WILLIAMS P

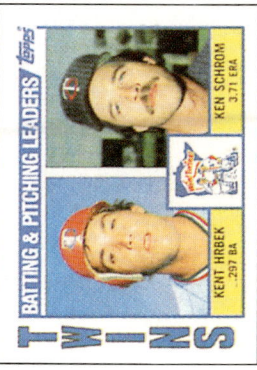

1985

A new owner, the return of the popular Bert Blyleven and some exciting hitters helped generate a club record 1,651,814 attendance but the fourth-place finish (77-85) was a bit of a disappointment. Second on May 21, the Twins lost 10 straight and never seriously challenged again. On June 21 Billy Gardner was fired and Ray Miller became the manager. The team was 50-50 under Miller.

Kirby Puckett hit .288 with 21 stolen bases. Kent Hrbek (.278) hit 21 homers and had 93 RBIs as the Twins' attack was helped by the cozy confines and light atmosphere of the Metrodome. Tom Brunansky (.242) hit 27 homers with 90 RBIs and Gary Gaetti (.246) added 20 homers and 63 RBIs. Blyleven returned on Aug. 1 from Cleveland and was 8-5 down the stretch to finish 17-16 overall. Frank Viola was 18-14, Mike Smithson 15-14, John Butcher 11-14 and Ron Davis (2-6) had 25 saves.

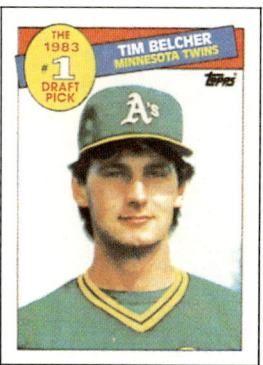

JOHN BUTCHER

BOBBY CASTILLO

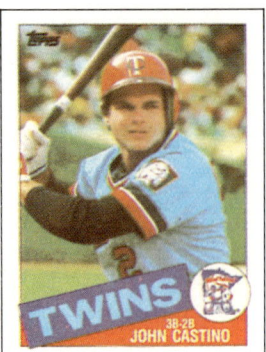
JOHN CASTINO

ANDRE DAVID

RON DAVIS

DAVE ENGLE

PETE FILSON

GARY GAETTI

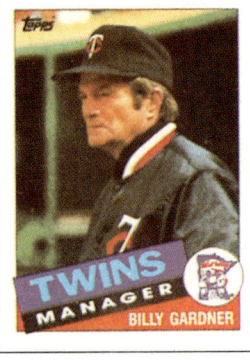
BILLY GARDNER

MICKEY HATCHER

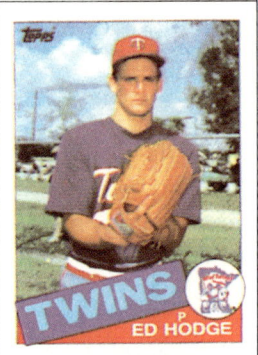
ED HODGE

KENT HRBEK

HOUSTON JIMENEZ

TIM LAUDNER

RICK LYSANDER

DAVE MEIER

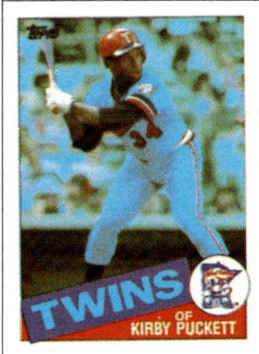

TWINS — KIRBY PUCKETT — OF

TWINS — PAT PUTNAM — 1B

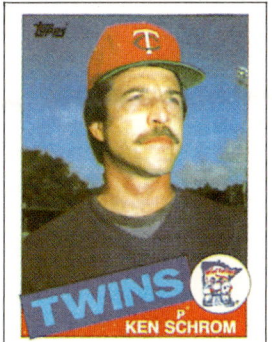

TWINS — KEN SCHROM — P

TWINS — MIKE SMITHSON — P

TWINS — CHRIS SPEIER — SS

TWINS — TIM TEUFEL — 2B

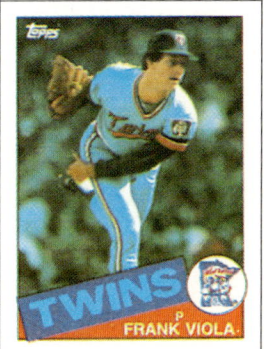

TWINS — FRANK VIOLA — P

FRANK VIOLA — LEFT-HANDED PITCHER — AL — ALL STAR

TWINS — MIKE WALTERS — P

TWINS — RON WASHINGTON — SS-2B

TWINS — LEN WHITEHOUSE — P

TWINS — AL WILLIAMS — P

1986

For the first time since 1964, the Twins had 5 men with 20 or more home runs but the season produced a generally uninspiring sixth-place finish (71-91), 21 games behind division-leading California. Manager Ray Miller was fired and Tom Kelly named interim manager on Sept. 12 but the team still missed fifth by 1 game.

Kirby Puckett, who hit .396 in April with 8 homers, had a superb all-around season. He batted .328, was second in the league in slugging (.537), runs (119) and hits (223) with 31 homers and 96 RBIs. Gary Gaetti (.287) had 34 homers (third in the league), Kent Hrbek (.267) had 29, Tom Brunansky (.256) had 23 and Roy Smalley (.246) had 20. Gaetti drove in 108 runs and Hrbek 91.

Bert Blyleven (17-14) led the league in innings pitched, was second in complete games (16) and fourth in strikeouts (215) in spite of a 4.01 ERA. Frank Viola was 16-13 and Mike Smithson was 13-14. Keith Atherton (5-8) led the relievers with 10 saves.

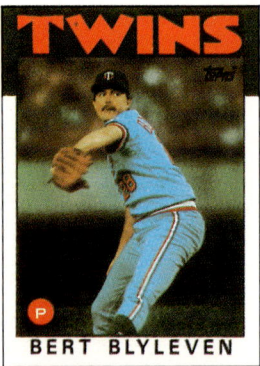
BERT BLYLEVEN

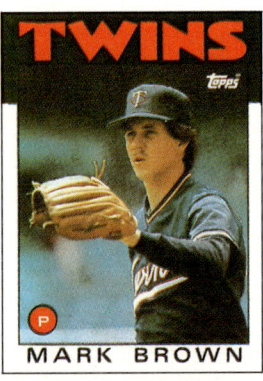
MARK BROWN

TOM BRUNANSKY

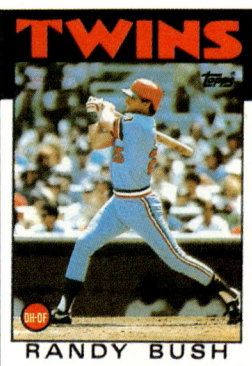
RANDY BUSH

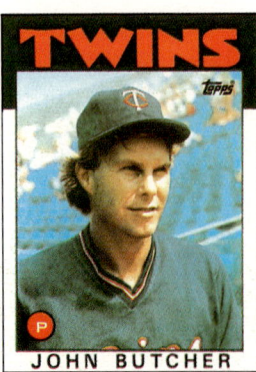
JOHN BUTCHER

RON DAVIS

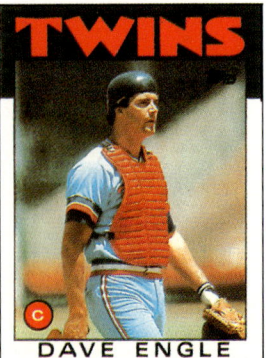
DAVE ENGLE

FRANK EUFEMIA

PETE FILSON

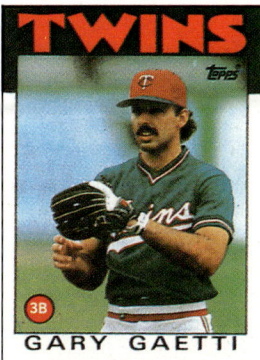
GARY GAETTI

TWINS 3B-SS GREG GAGNE

GREG GAGNE

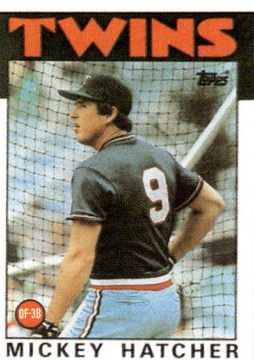
MICKEY HATCHER

KENT HRBEK

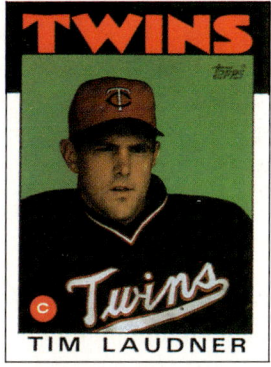
TIM LAUDNER

RICK LYSANDER

RAY MILLER

KIRBY PUCKETT

TWINS MARK SALAS

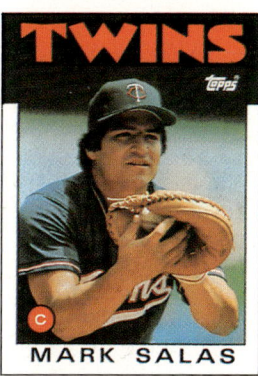
MARK SALAS

KEN SCHROM

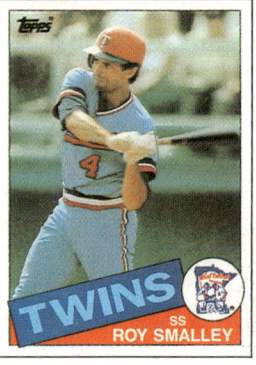
TWINS SS ROY SMALLEY

ROY SMALLEY

MIKE SMITHSON

MIKE STENHOUSE

DH-OF
MIKE STENHOUSE

TIM TEUFEL

FRANK VIOLA

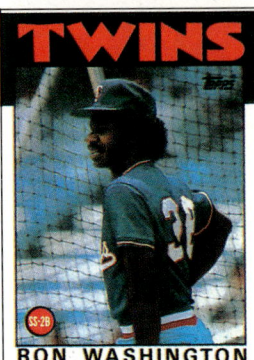

RON WASHINGTON

TWINS LEADERS

1987

There are no handy words to describe what the Minnesota Twins did in 1987. Try fantastic. Maybe unbelievable. Or just plain wonderful.

Whatever the choice of adjectives, the Twins thrilled 2,081,976 record-setting fans who poured into the Hubert Humphrey Metrodome to watch just about the best darn home-field team around.

At the finish, the Twins won the American League pennant for the first time in 22 years and the World Series for the first time ever.

When switch-hitting Gene Larkin was called up from the minors, the Twins made headlines for having the first player in the major leagues from Columbia University since Lou Gehrig played his final game in May 1939.

Many thought that would be the big story for the Twins' season. They were wrong.

Minnesota went into first place on July 6 and was there for all but three days the rest of the season. By late September, the Twins were serious news. On September 27, the Twins scored five times in the first inning (helped by three homers) and routed Kansas City, 8-1. The next night, it was Steve Lombardozzi with a three-run homer and a two-out RBI single in the eighth producing a 5-3 win at Texas that clinched the division. The Twins had won eight of 10 to close it out.

Then came the play-offs against the favored Detroit Tigers. The Twins won it in five games.

In the World Series, the Twins won all four games at the Metrodome to defeat the St. Louis Cardinals. An 11-5 rout in game six forced a decisive seventh game and Minnesota won that, 4-2, behind starter Frank Viola and reliever Jeff Reardon who allowed the Cards just six hits.

Viola was the hero of the pitching staff during the season, with a 17-10 record and a 2.90 ERA, the best in the league. Reardon had 31 saves in his first season with the Twins.

Bert Blyleven was 15-12 and Juan Berenguer 8-1 including the clinching at Texas on September 28.

Kirby Puckett was the most consistent hitter with a .332 average (fourth best in the league), with 28 homers and 99 RBI. Gary Gaetti had 31 homers and 109 RBI, giving him two straight years over the 30-homer, 100-RBI marks.

Kent Hrbek hit .285 with 34 homers and 90 RBI while Tom Brunansky added 32 homers and 85 RBI as the middle four hitters in the lineup hit 125 homers.

Gene Larkin? He hit .266 and had a big RBI double in the fourth game of the play-offs against the Tigers.

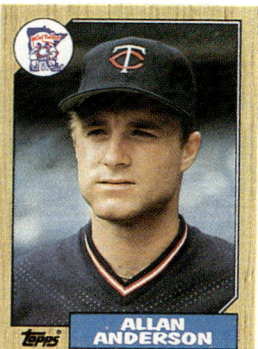
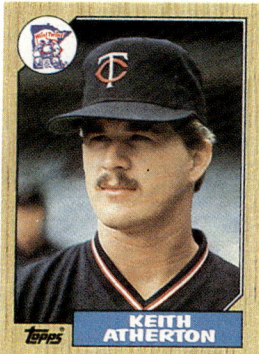
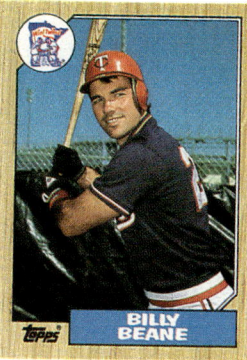
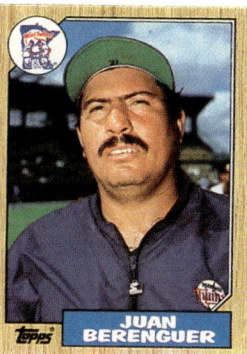

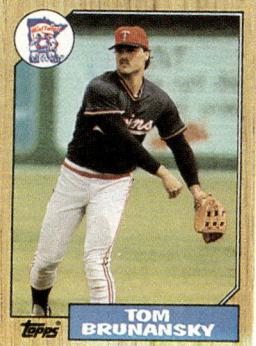

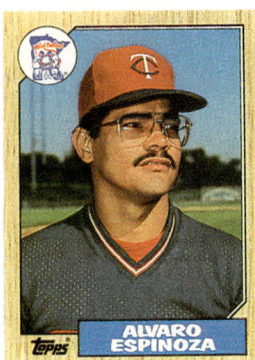

ALVARO
ESPINOZA

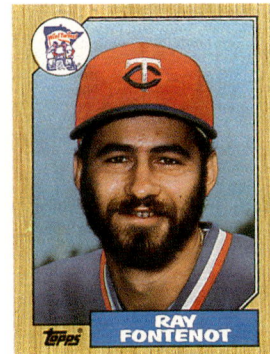

RAY
FONTENOT

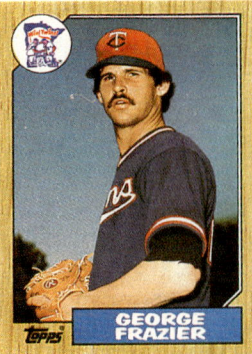

GEORGE
FRAZIER

GARY
GAETTI

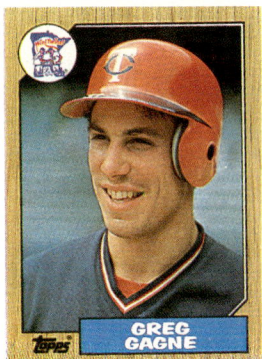

GREG
GAGNE

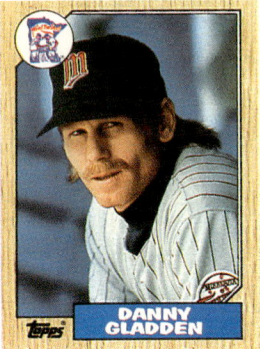

DANNY
GLADDEN

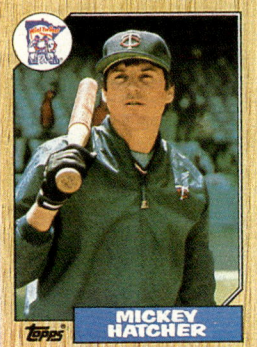

MICKEY
HATCHER

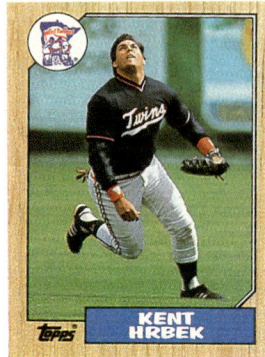

KENT
HRBEK

ROY LEE
JACKSON

TOM
KELLY

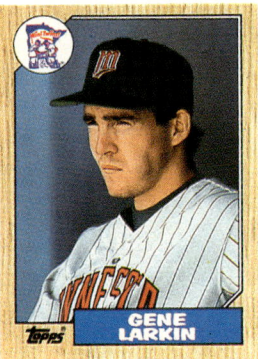

GENE
LARKIN

TIM
LAUDNER

STEVE
LOMBARDOZZI

AL
NEWMAN

JOE
NIEKRO

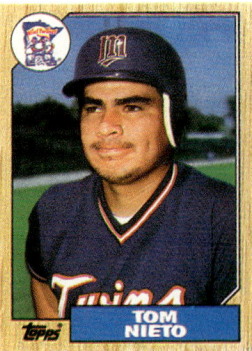

TOM
NIETO

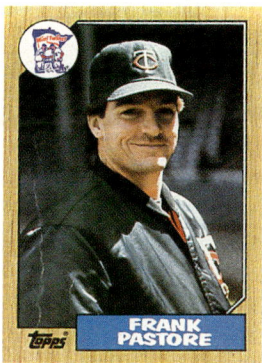

FRANK PASTORE

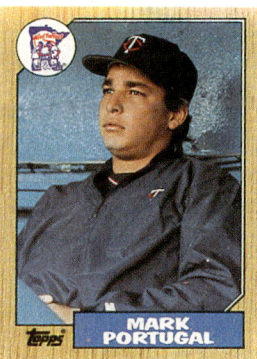

MARK PORTUGAL

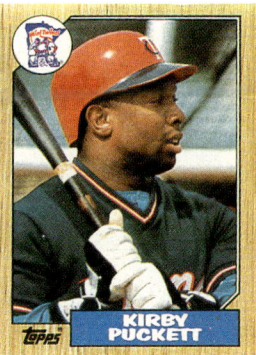

KIRBY PUCKETT

KIRBY PUCKETT
ALL STAR

JEFF REARDON

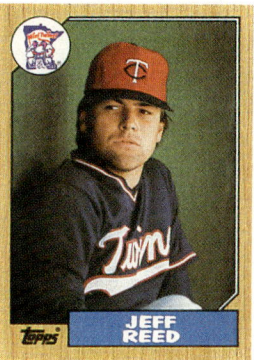

JEFF REED

MARK SALAS

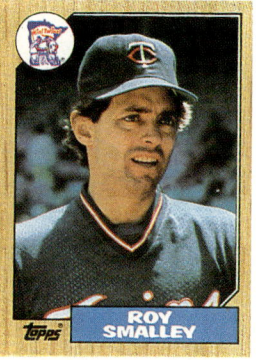

ROY SMALLEY

MIKE SMITHSON

LES STRAKER

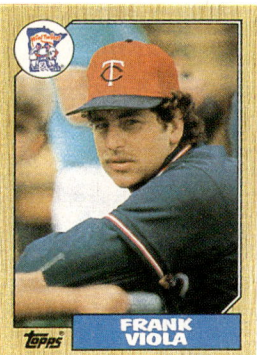

FRANK VIOLA

RON WASHINGTON

TWINS LEADERS

1988

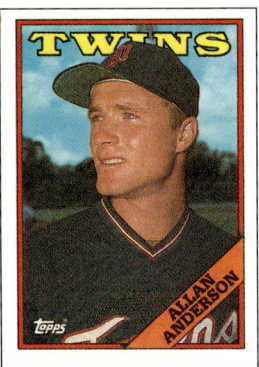
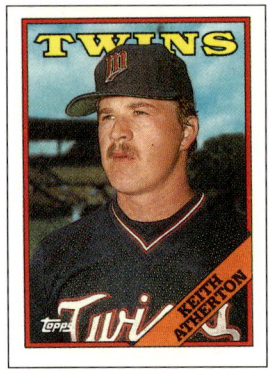

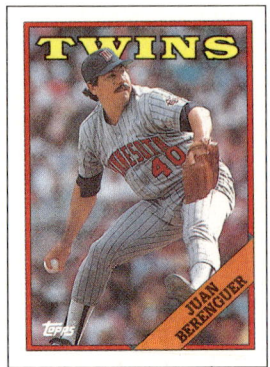

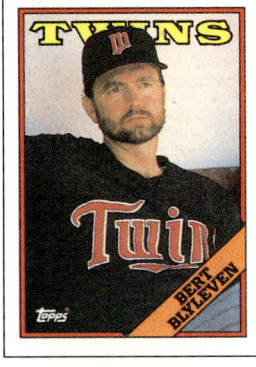
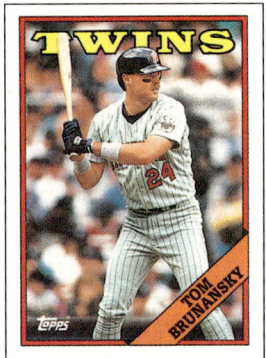
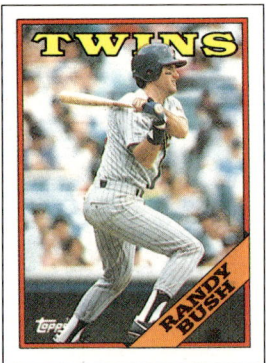
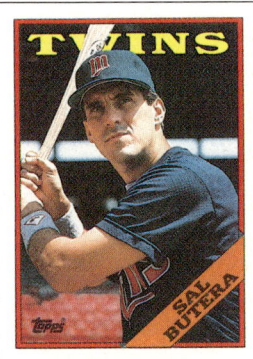

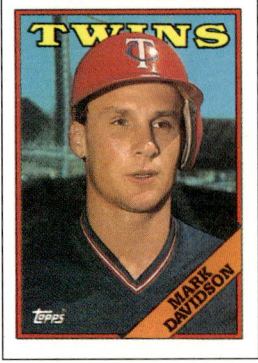
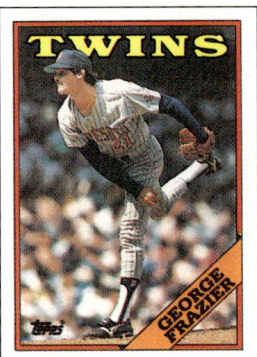
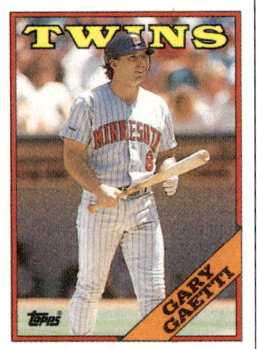
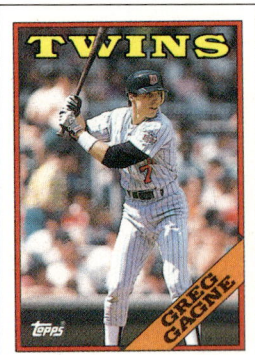

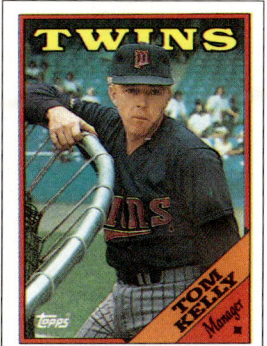

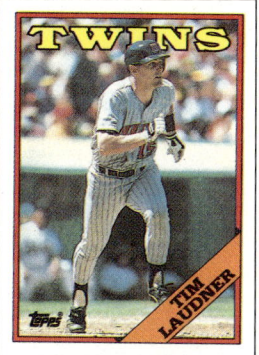
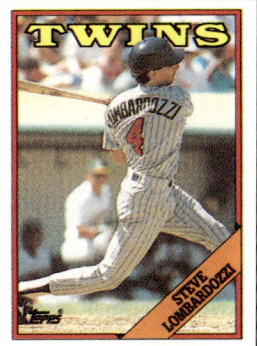
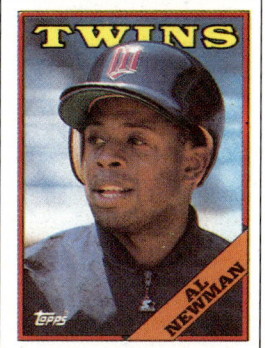

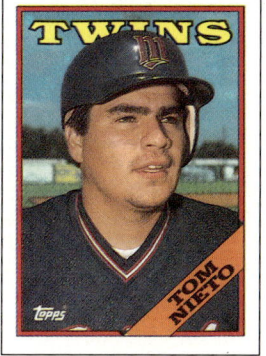
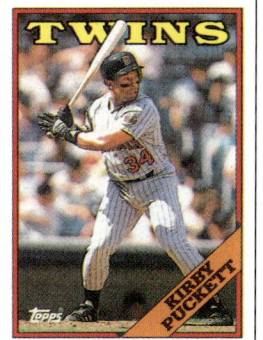

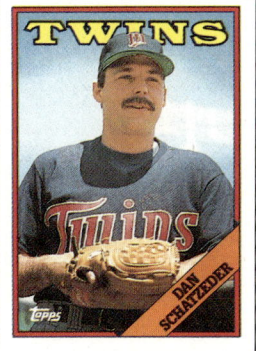
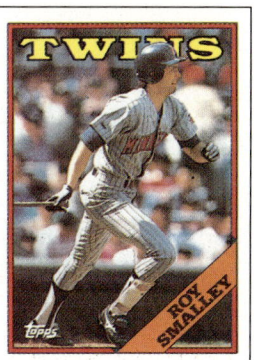

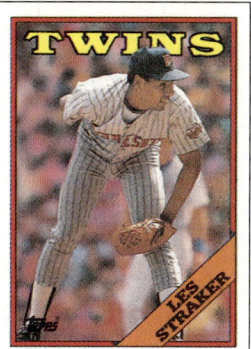

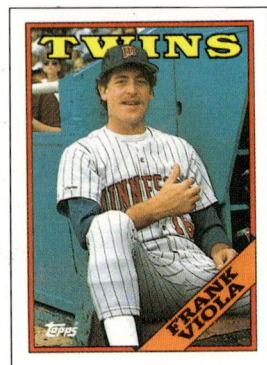

HARMON KILLEBREW

MINNESOTA 1st BASE-DH

HARMON KILLEBREW TWINS

Harmon Killebrew, number five on the all-time home run list, owns the American League record for such career endeavors with 573 home runs.

A member of the Hall of Fame since 1984, the ever-popular Killebrew seven times paced the American League in four-baggers and on nine occasions exceeded 100 RBIs in a season.

It was a U.S. senator from Idaho, the late Herman Welker, who tipped the then-Washington Senators to Killebrew's prowess. They made him a teenage bonus signee in 1954. The then-existing bonus rule in baseball compelled the former Idaho schoolboy slugger to spend nearly three years on the Washington bench and after some schooling in the Senators' farm system, Killebrew blossomed in 1959 when he hit 42 home runs to tie Cleveland's Rocky Colavito for the four-base title.

The franchise shift from Washington to Minnesota in 1961 proved more than beneficial to Killebrew. He launched the Midwest segment of his career by hitting 46 homers. His booming bat and pleasant personality made the youngster a folk hero in the upper Midwest.

Initially signed as a second baseman, the burly Killebrew played first and third bases, the outfield and in his later years assayed the designated hitter's role. Harmon hit 40 or more homers no fewer than eight times. From 1962-1964 he won the four-base title, averaging 47.3 home runs over that span.

Many baseball purists regarded him as an all-or-nothing-at-all slugger. Never a contender for the batting title, the solidly built slugger was paid for his ability to play long ball and he didn't short change his employers.

In the decade from 1960-1969, his 393 homers were the most by a hitter in either league. In 1969, a year he helped the Twins gain the American League's Western Division title, he was named the A.L.'s Most Valuable Player.

Despite 1,699 strikeouts, which places him ninth on a roster on which he follows such accomplished sluggers as Reggie Jackson, Mickey Mantle and Mike Schmidt, Harmon drew 1,559 walks, exceeding such as Lou Gehrig, Willie Mays, Jimmie Foxx and Henry Aaron in that regard.

Killebrew, without question made his base hits count. For instance, in 1959 he had 132 hits, 42 of which were home runs. In 1962 he had 134 safeties, including 48 homers. The following year it was 45 homers on 133 hits and in 1967 it was 44 homers on 147 base hits.

1951: Blue Back of Johnny Mize (50) lists for $25 . . . Red Back of Duke Snider (38) lists for $18 . . . Complete set of 9 Team Cards lists for $900 . . . Complete set of 11 Connie Mack All-Stars lists for $2750 with Babe Ruth and Lou Gehrig listing for $700 each . . . Current All-Stars of Jim Konstanty, Robin Roberts and Eddie Stanky list for $4000 each . . . Complete set lists for $14,250.

1952: Mickey Mantle (311) is unquestionably the most sought-after post-war gum card, reportedly valued at $6,500-plus . . . Ben Chapman (391) is photo of Sam Chapman . . . Complete set lists in excess of $36,000.

1953: Mickey Mantle (82) and Willie Mays (244) list for $1,500 each . . . Set features first TOPPS card of Hall-of-Famer Whitey Ford (207) and only TOPPS card of Hall-of-Famer Satchel Paige (220). Pete Runnels (219) is photo of Don Johnson . . . Complete set lists for $9,500.

1954: Ted Williams is depicted on two cards (1 and 250) . . . Set features rookie cards of Hank Aaron (128), Ernie Banks (94) and Al Kaline (201) . . . Card of Aaron lists for $650 . . . Card of Willie Mays (90) lists for $200 . . . Complete set lists for $5,500.

1955: Set features rookie cards of Sandy Koufax (123), Harmon Killebrew (124) and Roberto Clemente (164) . . . The Clemente and Willie Mays (194) cards list for $425 each . . .Complete set lists for $3,900.

1956: Set features rookie cards of Hall-of-Famers Will Harridge (1), Warren Giles (2), Walter Alston (8) and Luis Aparicio (292) . . . Card of Mickey Mantle (135) lists for $650 . . . Card of Willie Mays (130) lists for $125 . . . Complete set lists for $4,000 . . . The Team Cards are found both dated (1955) and undated and are valued at $15 (dated) and more . . . There are two unnumbered Checklist Cards valued high.

1957: Set features rookie cards of Don Drysdale (18), Frank Robinson (35) and Brooks Robinson (328) . . . A reversal of photo negative made Hank Aaron (20) appear as a left-handed batter . . . Card of Mickey Mantle (95) lists for $600 . . . Cards of Brooks Robinson and Sandy Koufax (302) list for $275 each . . . Complete set lists for $4,800.

1958: Set features first TOPPS cards of Casey Stengel (475) and Stan Musial (476) . . . Mike McCormick (37) is photo of Ray Monzant . . . Milt Bolling (188) is photo of Lou Berberet . . . Bob Smith (226) is photo of Bobby Gene Smith . . . Card of Mickey Mantle (150) lists for $400 . . . Card of Ted Williams (1) lists for $325 . . . Complete set lists for $4,800.

1959: In a notable error, Lou Burdette (440) is shown posing as a left-handed pitcher . . . Set features rookie card of Bob Gibson (514) . . . Ralph Lumenti (316) is photo of Camilo Pascual . . . Card of Gibson lists for $200 . . . Card of Mickey Mantle (10) lists for $300 . . . Complete set lists for $3,000.

1960: A run of 32 consecutively numbered rookie cards (117-148) includes the first card of Carl Yastrzemski (148) . . . J.C. Martin (346) is photo of Gary Peters . . . Gary Peters (407) is photo of J.C. Martin . . . Card of Yastrzemski lists for $150 . . . Card of Mickey Mantle (350) lists for $300 . . . Complete set lists for $2,600.

1961: The Warren Spahn All-Star (589) should have been numbered 587 . . . Set features rookie cards of Billy Williams (141) and Juan Marichal (417) . . . Dutch Dotterer (332) is photo of his brother, Tommy . . . Card of Mickey Mantle (300) lists for $200 . . . Card of Carl Yastrzemski (287) lists for $90 . . . Complete set lists for $3,600.

1962: Set includes special Babe Ruth feature (135-144) . . . some Hal Reniff cards numbered 139 should be 159 . . . Set features rookie card of Lou Brock (387) . . . Gene Freese (205) is shown posing as a left-handed batter . . . Card of Mickey Mantle (200) lists for $325 . . . Card of Carl Yastrzemski (425) lists for $125 . . . Complete set lists for $3,300.

1963: Set features rookie card of Pete Rose (537), which lists for $500-plus . . . Bob Uecker (126) is shown posing as a left-handed batter . . . Don Landrum (113) is photo of Ron Santo . . . Eli Grba (231) is photo of Ryne Duren . . . Card of Mickey Mantle (200) lists for $200 . . . Card of Lou Brock (472) lists for $75 . . . Complete set lists for $2,900.

1964: Set features rookie cards of Richie Allen (243), Tony Conigliaro (287) and Phil Niekro (541) . . . Lou Burdette is again shown posing as a left-handed pitcher . . . Bud Bloomfield (532) is photo of Jay Ward . . . Card of Pete Rose (125) lists for $150 . . . Card of Mickey Mantle (50) lists for $175 . . . Complete set lists for $1,600.

1965: Set features rookie cards of Dave Johnson (473), Steve Carlton (477) and Jim Hunter (526) . . . Lew Krausse (462) is photo of Pete Lovrich . . . Gene Freese (492) is again shown posing as a left-handed batter . . . Cards of Carlton and Pete Rose (207) list for $135 . . . Card of Mickey Mantle (350) lists for $300 . . . Complete set lists for $800.

1966: Set features rookie card of Jim Palmer (126) . . . For the third time (see 1962 and 1965) Gene Freese (319) is shown posing as a left-handed batter . . . Dick Ellsworth (447) is photo of Ken Hubbs (died February 13, 1964) . . . Card of Gaylord Perry (598) lists for $175 . . . Card of Willie McCovey (550) lists for $80 . . . Complete set lists for $2,500.

1967: Set features rookie cards of Rod Carew (569) and Tom Seaver (581) . . . Jim Fregosi (385) is shown posing as a left-handed batter . . . George Korince (72) is photo of James Brown but was later corrected on a second Korince card (526) . . . Card of Carew lists for $150 . . . Card of Maury Wills (570) lists for $65 . . . Complete set lists for $2,500.

1968: Set features rookie cards of Nolan Ryan (177) and Johnny Bench (247) . . . The special feature of The Sporting News All-Stars (361-380) includes eight players in the Hall of Fame . . . Card of Ryan lists for $135 . . . Card of Bench lists for $125 . . . Complete set lists for $1,200.

1969: Set features rookie card of Reggie Jackson (260) . . . There are two poses each for Clay Dalrymple (151) and Donn Clendenon (208) . . . Aurelio Rodriguez (653) is photo of Lenny Garcia (Angels' bat boy) . . . Card of Mickey Mantle (500) lists for $150 . . . Card of Jackson lists for $175 . . . Complete set lists for $1,200.

1970: Set features rookie cards of Vida Blue (21), Thurman Munson (189) and Bill Buckner (286) . . . Also included are two deceased players Miguel Fuentes (88) and Paul Edmondson (414) who died after cards went to press . . . Card of Johnny Bench (660) lists for $75 . . . Card of Pete Rose (580) lists for $75 . . . Complete set lists for $1,000.

1971: Set features rookie card of Steve Garvey (341) . . . the final series (644-752) is found in lesser quantity and includes rookie card (664) of three pitchers named Reynolds (Archie, Bob and Ken) . . . Card of Garvey lists for $65 . . . Card of Pete Rose (100) lists for $45 . . . Complete set lists for $1,000.

1972: There were 16 cards featuring photos of players in their boyhood years . . . Dave Roberts (91) is photo of Danny Coombs . . . Brewers Rookie Card (162) includes photos of Darrell Porter and Jerry Bell, which were reversed . . . Cards of Steve Garvey (686) and Rod Carew (695) list for $60 . . . Card of Pete Rose (559) lists for $50 . . . Complete set lists for $1,000.

1973: A special Home Run Card (1) depicted Babe Ruth, Hank Aaron and Willie Mays . . . Set features rookie card of Mike Schmidt (615) listing for $175 . . . Joe Rudi (360) is photo of Gene Tenace . . . Card of Pete Rose (130) lists for $18 . . . Card of Reggie Jackson (255) lists for $12.50 . . . Complete set lists for $600.

1974: Set features 15 San Diego Padres cards printed as "Washington, N.L." due to report of franchise move, later corrected . . . Also included was a 44-card Traded Series which updated team changes . . . Set features rookie card of Dave Winfield (456) . . . Card of Mike Schmidt (283) lists for $35 . . . Card of Winfield lists for $25 . . . Complete set lists for $325.

1975: Herb Washington (407) is the only card ever published with position "designated runner," featuring only base-running statistics . . . Set features rookie cards of Robin Yount (223), George Brett (228), Jim Rice (616), Gary Carter (620) and Keith Hernandez (623) . . . Don Wilson (455) died after cards went to press (January 5, 1975) . . . Card of Brett lists for $50 . . . Cards of Rice and Carter list for $35 . . . Complete set lists for $475 . . . TOPPS also tested the complete 660-card series in a smaller size (2¼ " x 3 1/8") in certain areas of USA in a limited supply . . . Complete set of "Mini-Cards" lists for $700.

1976: As in 1974 there was a 44-card Traded Series . . . Set features five Father & Son cards (66-70) and ten All-Time All-Stars (341-350) . . . Card of Pete Rose (240) lists for $15 . . . Cards of Jim Rice (340), Gary Carter (441) and George Brett (19) list for $12 . . . Complete set lists for $225.

1977: Set features rookie cards of Andre Dawson (473) and Dale Murphy (476) . . . Reuschel Brother Combination (634) shows the two (Paul and Rick) misidentified . . . Dave Collins (431) is photo of Bob Jones . . . Card of Murphy lists for $65 . . . Card of Pete Rose (450) lists for $8.50 . . . Complete set lists for $250.

1978: Record Breakers (1-7) feature Lou Brock, Sparky Lyle, Willie McCovey, Brooks Robinson, Pete Rose, Nolan Ryan and Reggie Jackson . . . Set features rookie cards of Jack Morris (703), Lou Whitaker (704), Paul Molitor/Alan Trammell (707), Lance Parrish (708) and Eddie Murray (36) . . . Card of Murray lists for $35 . . . Card of Parrish lists for $35 . . . Complete set lists for $200.

1979: Bump Wills (369) was originally shown with Blue Jays affiliation but later corrected to Rangers . . . Set features rookie cards of Ozzie Smith (116), Pedro Guerrero (719), Lonnie Smith (722) and Terry Kennedy (724) . . . Larry Cox (489) is photo of Dave Rader . . . Card of Dale Murphy (39) lists for $8 . . . Cards of Ozzie Smith and Eddie Murray (640) list for $7.50 . . . Complete set lists for $135.

1980: Highlights (1-6) feature Hall-of-Famers Lou Brock, Carl Yastrzemski, Willie McCovey and Pete Rose . . . Set features rookie cards of Dave Stieb (77), Rickey Henderson (482) and Dan Quisenberry (667) . . . Card of Henderson lists for $28 . . . Card of Dale Murphy (274) lists for $5.50 . . . Complete set lists for $135.

1981: Set features rookie cards of Fernando Valenzuela (302), Kirk Gibson (315), Harold Baines (347) and Tim Raines (479) . . . Jeff Cox (133) is photo of Steve McCatty . . . John Littlefield (489) is photo of Mark Riggins . . . Card of Valenzuela lists for $7.50 . . . Card of Raines lists for $9 . . . Complete set lists for $80.

1982: Pascual Perez (383) printed with no position on front lists for $35, later corrected . . . Set features rookie cards of Cal Ripken (21), Jesse Barfield (203), Steve Sax (681) and Kent Hrbek (766) . . . Dave Rucker (261) is photo of Roger Weaver . . . Steve Bedrosian (502) is photo of Larry Owen . . . Card of Ripken lists for $12.50 . . . Cards of Barfield and Sax list for $5 . . . Complete set lists for $75.

1983: Record Breakers (1-6) feature Tony Armas, Rickey Henderson, Greg Minton, Lance Parrish, Manny Trillo and John Wathan . . . A series of Super Veterans features early and current photos of 34 leading players . . . Set features rookie cards of Tony Gwynn (482) and Wade Boggs (498) . . . Card of Boggs lists for $32 . . . Card of Gwynn lists for $16 . . . Complete set lists for $85.

1984: Highlights (1-6) salute eleven different players . . . A parade of superstars is included in Active Leaders (701-718) . . . Set features rookie card of Don Mattingly (8) listing for $35 . . . Card of Darryl Strawberry (182) lists for $10 . . . Complete set lists for $85.

1985: A Father & Son Feature (131-143) is again included . . . Set features rookie cards of Scott Bankhead (393), Mike Dunne (395), Shane Mack (398), John Marzano (399), Oddibe McDowell (400), Mark McGwire (401), Pat Pacillo (402), Cory Snyder (403) and Billy Swift (404) as part of salute to 1984 USA Baseball Team (389-404) that participated in Olympic Games plus rookie cards of Roger Clemens (181) and Eric Davis (627) . . . Card of McGwire lists for $20 . . . Card of Davis lists for $18 . . . Card of Clemens lists for $11 . . . Complete set lists for $95.

1986: Set includes Pete Rose Feature (2-7), which reproduces each of Rose's TOPPS cards from 1963 thru 1985 (four per card) . . . Bob Rodgers (141) should have been numbered 171 . . . Ryne Sandberg (690) is the only card with TOPPS logo omitted . . . Complete set lists for $24.

1987: Record Breakers (1-7) feature Roger Clemens, Jim Deshaies, Dwight Evans, Davey Lopes, Dave Righetti, Ruben Sierra and Todd Worrell . . . Jim Gantner (108) is shown with Brewers logo reversed . . . Complete set lists for $22.

1988: Record Breakers (1-7) include Vince Coleman, Don Mattingly, Mark McGwire, Eddie Murray, Phil & Joe Niekro, Nolan Ryan and Benny Santiago. Al Leiter (18) was originally shown with photo of minor leaguer Steve George and later corrected. Complete set lists for $20.00.

Pitching Record & Index

PLAYER	G	IP	W	L	R	ER	SO	BB	GS	CG	SHO	SV	ERA
ABERNATHY, TED	681	1148	63	69			765	592	34	2	7	148	3.46
AGOSTO, JUAN	171	190.1	9	10	104	93	110	86	1	0	1	16	4.40
ALBURY, VIC	101	372	18	17			193	220	37	6	1	1	4.11
ANDERSON, ALLAN	21	84.1	3	6	54	52	51	30	10	1	0	0	5.55
ARRIGO, GERRY	194	620	35	40			433	291	80	9	3	4	5.21
ARROYO, FERNANDO	121	534	24	37			172	157	60	12	2	0	4.45
ATHERTON, KEITH	202	374	19	28	171	165	242	150	3	0	0	19	4.14
BACSIK, MIKE	73	173	8	6			77	75	25	0	0	2	4.42
BANE, ED	44	167	7	13			86	84	25	1	0	2	4.69
BEARDEN, GENE	193	789	45	38			259	435	84	29	7	1	3.96
BERENGUER, JUAN	183	645	30	41	324	287	498	335	86	5	2	5	4.00
BLACK, JOE	172	415	30	12			222	129	16	2	0	25	3.90
BLYLEVEN, BERT	541	3988	229	197	1532	1365	3090	1072	535	216	54	0	3.08
BONIKOWSKI, JOE	30	100	5	7			45	38	13	3	0	2	3.87
BORIS, PAUL	23	49.2	1	2			30	19	10	0	0	0	3.99
BOSWELL, DAVE	205	1065	68	56			882	481	151	37	6	0	3.52
BRANDON, DARRELL	228	590	28	37			354	275	43	7	2	13	4.04
BRETT, KEN	349	1526	83	85			807	562	184	51	8	11	3.93
BRODOWSKI, DICK	72	216	9	11			85	124	15	5	0	5	4.75
BROWN, MARK	15	38.2	1	2			15	14	0	0	0	0	5.12
BURGMEIER, TOM	745	1258.1	79	55			584	384	3	0	0	102	3.23
BUTCHER, JOHN	164	833.2	36	49	444	409	363	229	113	23	6	6	4.42
BUTLER, BILL	134	593	23	35			408	312	86	10	5	6	4.20
BYERLY, BUD	237	492	22	22			209	167	17	4	0	14	3.70
BYRNE, TOMMY	281	1363	85	69			766	1037	170	65	12	12	4.11
CAMPBELL, BILL	693	1219.2	83	68	538	475	860	491	9	2	1	126	3.51
CAMPISI, SAL	50	63	3	2			35	47	0	0	0	4	2.71
CARLTON, STEVE	705	5054.2	323	229	2000	1749	4040	1742	687	251	55	2	3.11
CARRITHERS, DON	165	565	28	32			275	267	67	11	3	3	4.46
CASTILLO, BOBBY	250	688.1	38	40			434	327	59	9	1	18	3.95
CHAKALES, BOB	171	420	15	25			187	225	23	3	1	10	4.54
CHANCE, DEAN	406	2148	128	115			1534	739	294	83	33	23	2.92
CICOTTE, AL	102	260	10	13			149	119	16	0	0	4	4.36
CIMINO, PETE	86	161	5	8			139	65	1	0	0	5	3.07
CLEVENGER, TEX	307	696	36	37			361	298	40	6	2	30	4.18
COLLUM, JACKIE	171	464	32	28			171	173	37	11	2	12	4.15
CONSTABLE, JIM	56	97	3	4			59	41	6	1	0	1	4.47
CONSUEGRA, SANDY	248	810	51	32			193	246	71	24	5	26	4.92
COOPER, DON	37	75.2	1	6			43	43	3	0	0	0	5.23
CORBETT, DOUG	302	530	24	28	206	184	327	187	1	0	0	65	3.37
CORBIN, RAY	181	652	36	38			248	261	63	12	3	17	3.12
CRIDER, JERRY	53	120	5	7			56	49	9	0	0	1	4.50
DAILEY, BILL	119	186	10	7			109	59	0	0	0	22	4.05
DAVIS, RON G.	447	692.1	46	52	324	303	550	276	2	0	0	130	3.94
DECKER, JOE	152	710	36	44			455	377	106	19	4	4	4.17
DONOHUE, JIM	70	156	3	4			116	82	9	0	0	7	4.27
DOTTER, GARY	7	12	0	0			10	7	0	0	0	0	5.25
ERICKSON, ROGER	135	799	35	53			365	251	117	24	5	1	4.13
EUFEMIA, FRANK	39	61.2	4	2			30	21	0	0	0	3	3.79
FELTON, TERRY	55	138.1	0	16			108	87	10	1	0	3	5.53
FERRICK, TOM	323	674	40	40			245	227	7	4	1	56	3.47
FIFE, DAN	14	57	3	2			21	33	7	1	0	0	5.37
FILSON, PETE	126	316.2	14	13			160	121	24	1	0	4	3.95
FISCHER, BILL	281	832	45	58			313	210	78	16	2	13	4.34
FONTENOT, RAY	145	493.2	25	26	253	221	216	153	62	3	1	2	4.03
FORNIELES, MIEK	432	1156	63	64			576	421	76	20	4	55	3.96

PLAYER	G	IP	W	L	R	ER	SO	BB	GS	CG	SHO	SV	ERA
FOSNOW, JERRY	36	58	3	4			44	33	0	0	0	2	5.59
FRAZIER, GEORGE	361	594.1	30	38			391	262	0	0	0	27	4.09
GEBHARD, BOB	31	41	1	3			26	24	2	0	0	1	5.93
GIEL, PAUL	30	57	1	1			32	32	2	0	0	1	5.21
GOLTZ, DAVE	353	2038.1	113	119			1105	646	264	83	13	8	3.69
GOMEZ, RUBEN	289	1453	76	86			677	574	205	63	15	5	4.09
GRANGER, WAYNE	451	640	35	35			303	201	0	0	0	108	3.14
GRANT, JIM	571	2441	145	119			1267	849	293	89	18	53	3.63
GRIGGS, HAL	105	348	6	26			172	209	45	6	1	3	5.48
GRZENDA, JOE	219	309	14	13			173	120	3	0	0	14	3.99
GUMPERT, RANDY	261	1052	51	59			352	346	113	47	6	7	4.17
HALL, TOM	358	854	52	33			797	382	63	7	3	32	3.27
HAMM, PETE	23	60	2	6			19	25	8	1	0	0	6.43
HANDS, BILL	374	1951	111	110			1098	492	260	72	17	14	3.35
HARRIS, LUM	151	819	35	63			232	265	91	46	4	3	4.16
HARRIS, MICKEY	271	1051	59	71			534	455	109	42	2	21	4.18
HARRISON, RORIC	140	590	30	35			319	257	70	12	1	10	4.24
HARRIST, EARL	132	383	12	28			162	193	24	2	0	10	4.34
HARTZELL, PAUL	170	703.1	27	39			237	181	87	22	2	12	3.90
HAVENS, BRAD	109	438	21	31			267	171	58	6	2	1	4.93
HAYDEL, HAL	35	49	6	2			33	24	0	0	0	1	4.04
HAYNES, JOE	379	1580	76	82			475	620	147	53	5	21	4.01
HERNANDEZ, RUDY	28	44	4	2			26	24	0	0	0	0	4.09
HODGE, ED	25	100	4	3			59	29	15	0	0	0	4.77
HOLLY, JEFF	39	89	3	4			49	33	6	0	0	0	5.66
HOWE, STEVE	212	307	23	24			172	69	0	0	0	56	2.17
HUDSON, SID	380	2181	104	152			734	835	279	123	11	13	4.28
HUGHES, JIM M.	76	441	25	30			226	205	62	16	2	0	4.31
HYDE, DICK	169	298	17	14			144	137	2	0	0	23	3.56
JACKSON, DARRELL	102	410.2	20	27			229	186	60	3	1	1	4.38
JACKSON, ROY LEE	280	559.1	28	34			351	203	18	1	0	34	3.77
JOHNSON, DAVE C.	53	109	4	10			56	34	7	0	0	2	4.62
JOHNSON, DON	198	631	27	38			262	285	70	17	4	12	4.78
JOHNSON, TOM	129	274	23	14			166	93	1	0	0	22	3.38
JOHNSON, WALTER	802	5926	416	279			3506	1404	666	532	112	36	2.17
KAAT, JIM	898	4527.2	283	237			2461	1083	625	180	31	18	3.45
KEMMERER, RUSS	302	1066	43	59			505	389	109	24	8	8	4.47
KLINE, RON	736	2078	114	144			989	731	203	44	8	108	3.86
KLIPPSTEIN, JOHNNY	711	1970	101	118			1158	978	162	37	6	66	4.24
KOOSMAN, JERRY	612	3839.1	222	209			2556	1198	527	140	33	17	3.36
KRALICK, JACK	235	1218	67	65			668	318	169	45	12	1	3.56
KUZAVA, BOB	213	862	49	44			446	415	99	34	5	13	4.05
LA ROCHE, DAVE	647	1049	65	58			819	459	15	1	0	126	3.53
LANE, JERRY	31	79	2	6			33	25	2	0	0	1	4.44
LASHER, FRED	151	202	11	13			148	110	1	0	0	22	3.88
LEE, DON	244	828	40	44			467	281	97	13	4	11	3.61
LEONARD, E. 'DUTCH'	640	3220	191	181			1170	737	375	192	30	44	3.25
LITTLE, JEFF	40	55.1	3	1			43	36	0	0	0	0	4.07
LUEBBER, STEVE	66	206	6	10			93	106	24	2	1	3	4.63
LUMENTI, RALPH	13	33	1	3			30	42	5	1	0	0	7.36
LYSANDER, RICK	137	256.2	9	17			111	96	5	1	0	11	4.28
MARANDA, GEORGES	49	124	2	7			64	65	8	1	0	4	4.50
MARRERO, CONNIE	118	735	39	40			297	249	94	51	7	3	3.67
MARSHALL, MIKE G.	723	1386	97	112			880	514	24	3	1	187	3.15
MASTERSON, WALT	399	1648	78	100			815	886	184	70	15	20	4.15

PLAYER

PLAYER	G	IP	W	L	R	ER	SO	BB	GS	CG	SHO	SV	ERA
MATHIAS, CARL	11	29	0	2			20	12	3	0		0	7.14
MCDERMOTT, MICKEY	291	1316	69	69			757	838	156	54	11	14	3.91
MCDEVITT, DANNY	155	456	21	27			303	264	60	13	4	7	4.40
MERRITT, JIM	297	1484	81	96			932	322	192	56	9	7	3.65
MILLER, BOB L.	694	1552	69	81			895	608	99	7	5	52	3.37
MOORE, RAY	365	1073	63	59			612	560	105	24	5	46	4.06
MORGAN, TOM	443	1025	67	47			364	300	61	18	7	64	3.60
MORRIS, DANNY	6	16	0	2			7	8	3	0	0	0	2.81
NELSON, MEL	93	174	4	10			98	69	11	1	0	5	4.40
NEWSOM, BOBO	600	3758	211	222			2082	1732	483	246	30	21	3.99
NIEKRO, JOE	670	3426	213	190	1506	1331	1656	1191	472	106	29	16	3.50
O'CONNOR, JACK	80	248.2	13	14			128	127	27	6	0	1	4.99
OELKERS, BRYAN	45	103.1	3	8	72	69	46	57	12	0	0	1	6.01
OGIER, MOE					No major league statistics								
OLLOM, JIM	24	45	0	1			28	12	3	0	0	0	5.00
PACELLA, JOHN	69	180.1	4	10			111	120	21	0	0	2	5.84
PASCUAL, CAMILO	529	2930	174	170			2167	1069	404	132	36	10	3.63
PASTORE, FRANK	220	986.1	48	58	507	470	541	301	139	22	7	6	4.29
PAZIK, MIKE	13	47	1	4			20	20	6	2	0	0	5.74
PEARCE, JIM	30	85	3	4			22	53	7	2	0	0	5.82
PERRANOSKI, RON	737	1176	79	74			687	468	1	0	0	179	2.79
PERRY, JIM	630	3287	215	174			1580	998	447	109	32	10	3.44
PERZANOWSKI, STAN	37	143	5	11			70	60	16	2	0	0	5.10
PLEIS, BILL	190	280	21	16			184	126	10	1	0	13	4.08
PORTERFIELD, BOB	318	1568	87	97			572	552	193	92	23	8	3.79
PORTUGAL, MARK	33	137	7	13	72	69	79	64	21	3	0	1	4.53
RAMOS, PEDRO	582	2355	117	160			1305	724	268	73	13	55	4.08
REARDON, JEFF	456	665.2	42	46	226	207	537	246	0	0	0	162	2.80
REDFERN, PETE	170	714.1	42	48			426	306	111	9	1	7	4.54
ROGGENBURK, GARRY	79	125	6	9			56	64	6	1	0	9	3.64
ROLAND, JIM	216	450	19	17			272	229	29	6	1	9	3.22
ROMONOSKY, JOHN	32	101	3	4			63	51	3	0	0	2	5.17
ROSS, BOB	20	48	0	2			29	38	3	0	0	1	7.13
SADOWSKI, TED	43	84	2	3			39	31	2	1	0	5	5.79
SANCHEZ, RAUL	49	90	5	3			48	43	2	1	1	1	4.60
SANDERS, KEN	408	657	29	45			360	258	1	0	0	86	2.97
SCARBOROUGH, RAY	318	1429	80	85			564	611	168	59	9	14	4.13
SCARCE, MAC	159	210	6	19			164	117	0	0	0	21	3.69
SCHATZEDER, DAN	328	1077	58	59			584	378	118	18	4	6	3.58
SCHEULER, RON	291	914	40	48			563	393	86	13	2	11	4.08
SCHMITZ, JOHNNY	366	1813	93	114			746	757	235	86	16	19	3.54
SCHROLL, AL	35	118	6	9			63	64	13	3	0	0	5.34
SCHROM, KEN	144	746.1	45	38	409	370	311	263	108	18	2	1	4.46
SERUM, GARY	62	271	10	12			125	74	28	6	1	1	4.72
SHEA, FRANK	195	944	56	46			361	497	118	48	12	5	3.79
SHELLENBACK, JIM	165	455	16	30			222	200	48	8	2	2	3.80
SIEBLER, DWIGHT	49	118	4	3			71	44	8	1	0	1	3.43
SIMA, AL	100	308	11	21			111	132	30	4	0	4	4.62
SINGER, BILL	322	2174	118	127			1515	781	308	96	24	2	3.39
SINGLETON, ELMER	145	327	11	17			160	146	19	2	1	4	4.84
SLEATER, LOU	131	301	12	18			152	172	21	7	1	5	4.69
SMITH, ROY	34	148.2	6	9			83	57	25	1	0	0	4.90
SMITHSON, MIKE	148	977	56	59			544	273	147	39	5	0	4.19
SPRING, JACK	155	186	12	5			86	78	5	0	0	8	4.26
STANFIELD, KEVIN	3	3	0	0			0	0	0	0	0	0	6.00
STANGE, LEE	359	1216	62	61			718	344	115	32	8	21	3.56
STEPHEN, BUZZ	2	11	1	1			4	7	2	0	0	0	4.91
STEWART, BUNKY	72	187	7	11			77	127	14	2	0	3	6.02
STIGMAN, DICK	235	923	46	54			755	406	119	30	5	16	4.03
STOBBS, CHUCK	459	1920	107	130			897	735	238	65	7	19	4.29
STONE, DEAN	215	687	29	39			380	373	85	19	5	12	4.47

PLAYER

PLAYER	G	IP	W	L	R	ER	SO	BB	GS	CG	SHO	SV	ERA
SULLIVAN, FRANK	351	1732	97	100			959	559	219	73	15	18	3.60
SUTTON, JOHNNY	31	68	2	1			27	24	0	0	0	1	3.57
THORMODSGARD, PAUL	50	285	12	21			118	82	49	9	1	0	4.74
TIANT, LUIS	573	3485.2	229	172			2416	1104	484	187	49	15	3.30
VALENTINETTI, VITO	108	257	13	14			94	122	15	3	0	3	4.73
VEINTIDOS, JUAN					No major league statistics								
VERHOEVEN, JOHN	99	204	3	8			90	63	0	0	0	4	3.79
VIOLA, FRANK	165	1090	63	64	591	530	689	354	164	33	6	0	4.38
VOSSLER, DAN					No major league statistics								
WALL, MURRAY	91	192	13	14			82	63	1	0	0	14	4.22
WALTERS, MIKE	46	88	1	4			31	34	0	0	0	4	3.99
WARDLE, CURT	52	119	8	9			89	62	12	0	0	1	6.13
WEIK, DICK	76	213	6	22			123	237	26	3	2	1	5.92
WHITBY, BILL	4	6	0	0			2	1	0	0	0	0	9.00
WHITEHOUSE, LEN	92	108	9	4			64	63	1	0	0	3	4.25
WIESLER, BOB	70	240	7	19			113	218	38	4	0	0	5.78
WILLIAMS, AL	120	642.2	35	38			262	227	97	15	1	2	4.24
WILLIAMS, STAN	482	1763	109	94			1305	748	208	42	11	43	3.48
WOODESHICK, HAL	427	847	44	62			484	389	62	7	1	61	3.56
WOODSON, DICK	137	589	34	32			315	253	76	15	5	2	3.47
WORTHINGTON, AL	602	1245	75	82			834	527	69	11	3	110	3.39
WYNN, EARLY	691	4566	300	244			2334	1775	612	290	49	15	3.54
YETT, RICH	40	79	5	3	49	46	50	39	4	1	0	1	5.24
ZAHN, GEOFF	304	1848.2	111	109			705	526	270	79	20	1	3.74
ZEPP, BILL	63	188	10	5			81	72	24	1	1	4	3.64